A SIMON & SCHUSTER TRAVEL GUIDE

FRANCE

Produced by
Lyle Kenyon Engel

Editorial Staff:
Rhoda Blumberg, Executive Editor
Marla Ray, Assistant Editor
George S. Engel, Picture Editor
Norman Monath, Production
Alice Koeth, Illustrations & Maps

PUBLISHED BY

CORNERSTONE LIBRARY, INC.

DISTRIBUTED BY SIMON & SCHUSTER, INC.
Rockefeller Center
630 Fifth Avenue, New York, N.Y. 10020

Sincerest thanks to:
The French Government Tourist Office
Pan American Airways
Varig Brazilian Airlines
Lufthansa German Airlines
for their help and cooperation
during the preparation of this book.

Manufactured in the United States of America
under the supervision of
Rolls Offset Printing Co. Inc. N.Y.

CONTENTS

Aerial view of Paris, the Seine, and the Eiffel tower, Paris, France.

Mont-Saint-Michel
Solitary island standing in the middle of its sands

FRANCE FOR YOU

France is a country of 212,918 square miles, and more than 50 million Frenchmen. It has 485,000 miles of roads, hundreds of beaches, ski resorts and spas. As a gourmet's Paradise it has attracted countless numbers who "travel on their stomachs" from one famous restaurant to another. Its many museums, chateaux and cathedrals make the past alive and the present enchanting.

Man's imagination has always dreamed of a machine to travel back through the ages. France is, in a way, such a machine. It is Caesar's Gaul and Eisenhower's Normandy, and long before—30,000 years ago—it was home to the men of prehistory whose drawings remain in the Lascaux caves, whose megaliths still rise in Brittany.

Through France is spread the history of Europe, as well as the history of France. In the ellipse of the arena at Nîmes, in the precision of the language, and in the conciseness of the laws, Rome lives in France today. At Carcassonne are towers built by the Visigoths. At Les Andelys is the "ultimate" fortress of Richard the Lion-Hearted. At Avignon is the residence of the Popes in exile. At Vincennes, England's Henry V died.

Versailles Palace, famed residence of French kings.

France blossomed in the Renaissance, and the Renaissance blooms still in the chateaux of the Loire. Mementos of a splendid century and a terrible revolution live on, as do echoes of Empire, reminders of the artistic and intellectual ferment of the beginnings of this century, the marks of three wars within three generations.

Yet France always proves resilient. The consequences of each artistic, religious, or political upheaval are somehow absorbed, and to the surprise of all—save the French—France continues much the same.

In contemplating the history and longevity of France, the Frenchman is the clue. He is a specialist in the art of survival—survival of the individual in the midst of the group, be it at peace or at war. Connoisseur of the secret ways of the mind and the heart, he both asserts and protects his individuality by apparent paradox. In him you will find an enigmatic juxtaposition of emotion and logic, a seeming conflict between generosity and avarice, idealism and cynicism, passion and apathy, sentiment and realism, gaiety and shrewdness. French *politesse* is a veneer that may at first charm you, then exasperate you, for its basis is not friendliness, but reserve. With time, patience, perseverance, you may see beyond, into the intricate depths of French personality, which include warmth, wit, and loyalty. Lacking the time or inclination to uncover more than a few facets, you may, however, find the French character provocative, puzzling, and contradictory. Only in terms of American openness is it so. Through *politesse*, the French strive to protect the bases for their survival—their seriousness, their thrift, their regard for privacy.

Whether you care to prove the personality or not, you are free to enjoy the fruits of its nature. Most important is a profound sense of continuity which permits a savoring of the present that other cultures do not often allow. *Le bel aujourd'hui*—the beautiful today—is, perhaps, the most glorious experience that France can offer. In France, the present appears in perspective. It is neither an insignificant appendage to the past nor a temporary threshold to the future, but a thoroughly respectable moment in itself, sufficiently important to be treated with consideration.

This beautifully sculptured fountain in the garden, Le Luxembourg, is usually frequented by many students, Paris, France.

Because the present receives its due, France is a country to delight the senses, to enchant the eye, the ear, the palate. Time is taken to appreciate the pleasures of today—a meal, a view, a conversation. In *le bel aujourd'hui* there is always time to enjoy, to absorb, to reflect, even simply to be quiet.

Visitors to France often feel an urgency to seek out the past. But France is not a sleeping beauty, despite its wealth of historical association. It is past and present all in one. To be conscious of this unity is to realize that France is a gift of time. To accept this gift is to receive the country's most spectacular offering.

The France you will find depends in part upon yourself. The length of your journey has less to do with it than the tempo.

If your visit to France is a dash from cathedral to chateau to museum you will see a great deal, but you will not see modern France. Sit in a park or café, walk in cities and villages, picnic in the countryside. There is no guided tour to *le bel aujourd'hui*, but it is everywhere in France for you to discover for yourself.

What To Know Before You Go. France is the foreign country that most Americans most want to see. There's good reason. It's different enough to be "foreign," but not so different that you will lose your bearings completely and feel disoriented. Alfred North Whitehead summed it up perfectly in these words:

"A diversification among human communities is essential for the provision of the incentive and material for the Odyssey of the human spirit. Other nations of different habits are not enemies; they are godsends. Men require of their neighbors something sufficiently akin to be understood, something sufficiently different to provoke attention, and something great enough to command admiration."

You will find these things in France.

How to Get There. Jet planes and ships connect France with all parts of the world. Choose a jet if time is limited, or cross the Atlantic by ship if your schedule permits.

There are many air fare structures on the trans-Atlantic airline routes: first class, economy class, peak season, shoulder season,

Young artist sketches the bridge, Le Pont Des Arts, which spans the Seine river, Paris, France.

and low season—all with separate fare structures. There are also special fares based on your length of stay, usually referred to as "Excursion Fares." There are special Youth Fares, group discount plans and charter flights. Your travel agent or airline personnel will guide you in finding the appropriate fare for your trip to France.

When Should You Go? Anytime. The climate is temperate, never as hot as New York or the Midwest can get, never as cold. Though France is a bit more northerly than most of the United States, its weather is tempered by the Gulf Stream, so it seldom experiences our extremities of climate. Above 80° or below 35° is very unusual weather for Paris. In the south of France, of course, it may get a bit hotter; in the Alpine resorts, colder—but that's why you go there.

Passports and Visas? For a stay of less than three months, you need only have a valid U. S. passport.

Citizens of other countries should check with the local authorities on regulations governing the application for a passport.

When's High Season? Depends on where you're going and why. High season for American vacations to Europe is June through August. High season in Paris is May through August, though off-season designations differ widely. High season in the Alpine and other mountain resorts, of course, is just the opposite . . . December through February. Wherever in France you want to go, and whenever, check to see if off-season rates apply. If they do, you may save as much as 30 per cent.

What To Take? As little as you can—the theory is never to take more than you yourself can carry. If you fly, your baggage limitations are 66 pounds in first-class, 44 pounds in tourist. Excess baggage will cost you quite a bit extra—and probably won't be worth either the price or the bother. For Paris and the larger cities, dress as you would in New York, Chicago, or San Francisco—your chic and pretty big-city clothes. Black, of

Formal salon decorated in the Empire style of Napoleonic era,
Malmaison, near Paris.

course, is always good for big-city wear. For men, city or going-to-the-office attire is recommended. Flat sandals and sports shirts are as out of style in Paris as they would be in New York. If you're going to a big resort, take your newest and most attractive clothes, geared for the type of activity you're after—skiing, swimming, dancing, dining. Other guidebooks may caution women to take their "most comfortable shoes." Yes, take something you can walk in for hours—but don't limit your shoe wardrobe to flats. You'll want heels too, to compete with the well-shod Parisiennes. If you plan to go to a major summer resort—and participate in the major night life—take a dinner jacket and an evening dress. This should also be done if you plan to go to any of the Paris galas—at the Opera or elsewhere. Otherwise, you won't need them. If you're going to France in the winter, take warm dresses, bathrobes, and suits. Although it doesn't get freezing cold outside, it may seem very chilly inside. If you plan to be in the mountains anytime, take a topcoat or heavy sweaters. If you're heading for a Mediterranean resort, and are proud of your figure, take a bikini or buy one there. Otherwise, you'll be overdressed. On a Riviera beach, the one-piece bathing suit looks like grandma's bathing costume.

What About Electric Current? In most of France, current is 110-115 volts A. C., but 50-cycles, no 60-cycles as in the U. S. This means that electric equipment with moving parts (such as electric razors, phonographs, etc.) should be adjusted to function properly. Equipment without moving parts (radios, irons, etc.) will operate satisfactorily. Check with the manufacturer of your equipment. You will, in any case, need converter plugs, since plug-in sockets require a different type of prong.

What About Customs? You may bring into France 400 cigarettes, or 125 cigars, 2 bottles of liquor with the seals broken, and clothing for personal use. Also 2 still cameras of different size and make; 1 movie camera; 10 rolls or 12 plates of film for each still camera; 10 rolls of film for the movie camera; 1 portable musical instrument; 1 recording machine with 2 rolls of tape or wire or 10 records; 1 portable radio; 1 pair of binoculars, field or opera glasses; 1 portable typewriter; 1 set of sports equipment

A view of the Seine river from the top of Notre Dame Cathedral, Paris, France.

such as 1 tent, skis, tennis racket, gun. (Good luck to your 44 pounds if you have all that!) But before you leave the U.S., be sure to register with U.S. customs any item you have of foreign make, such as your watch or camera, so it will not be subject to duty when you return to the U.S.

Here, once again, for countries other than the United States, you should check with the local authorities for current customs regulations.

How Much Will It Cost? That depends entirely on you. Aside from your basic first-class or tourist air fare, the cost depends on your taste, your itinerary (Paris is more expensive than the provinces), your weakness for taxis, good food, high life. Generally, about $40 a day will see you through in comfort but not luxury, for everything except trans-Atlantic and city-to-city transportation. You can do it for as little as $10 a day if you're extremely careful, extremely knowledgeable and extremely open-minded about accommodations; or you can do it for $100 a day—or much more, if you want to. Unless you envision yourself as a youth hostler or a camper or a bona fide student or a real millionaire, figure on about $40 a day in Paris (not at a luxury hotel) and about $20 to $25 a day in the provinces—more if your province-time is spent at famous resorts, less if it's spent at relatively *untrammeled* places.

What About French Money? In France the unit of currency is the franc—usually written ''F.'' The official rate of exchange (as in the case in money markets throughout the world) is subject to fluctuation. We have used five Francs to the U.S. dollar in this book for purposes of stating approximate prices. French coins in common usage are 1, 2, 5, 10 and 20, in the centime range, and 1, 2, 5 and 20, in franc pieces. Banknotes come in denominations of 5, 10, 50, 100 and 500 F.

Should You Buy Francs Before You Leave? You'll find it handy to have about $10 or $20 worth of francs with you on your arrival in France, to take care of tips and taxis until you reach your first

Aerial view of the Seine with the Ile de St. Louis at right and the magnificent Hôtel De Ville in the foreground at left, Paris, France.

destination. You can buy them at your bank in the U. S. The only advantage of buying a small amount of francs before you leave is convenience.

How Should You Carry Your Money? In traveler's checks, by all means. Buy them at your bank. Some American credit cards are accepted in larger cities, but don't count on it. Almost anywhere, you'll have the devil's own time trying to cash a personal check. You can cash your traveler's checks at most hotels and restaurants, any French bank or exchange office, or American or British travel agency, for the official rate. Whoever cashes your traveler's checks deducts a small commission which may vary slightly from place to place.

How Can You Get About in France?
By Plane. Airlines connect the major cities. Service is reliable, fares are comparable to those in the U. S.

By Train. The French are justly proud of their French National Railways (S.N.C.F), which offer fast, efficient and dependable service over a vast network of lines. You can travel either first or second class. For overnight trips you can choose between first or second class "couchette" (berth) or first or second class Wagon-Lit. First class Wagon-Lit provides single or double roomettes. Second class Wagon-Lit and *couchettes* provide bunks, but less privacy. Overnight trains almost always have a dining car. The S.N.C.F. offers a staggering variety of services and rate-reductions. Ask your travel agent about them or write to the S.N.C.F. office at 610 Fifth Avenue, New York City. If you plan to travel much by train in Europe, look into the advantages of a *Eurailpass* which provides unlimited rail travel throughout Western Europe. You must purchase your Eurailpass before you leave the United States.

Tip: Always hang on to your train ticket. Tickets are collected as you leave the train at the end of your journey.

Spectacular palace of Versailles, fronted by li[...] in the night, near Paris, France.

By Bus. A great variety of bus tours and excursions are offered by the S.N.C.F., by the Regie Autonome des Transports Parisiens (R.A.T.P.), and other agencies. An extensive network of local bus services covers the entire country, making it possible to get to even the most remote areas.

By Car. France has more roads than any other country in the world of comparable size. Some are superhighways with heavy traffic, but more usual are the well-kept two-lane highways lined with trees. Driving in Paris can be nerve-wracking but elsewhere it can be a delightful way to see the country, particularly if you stick to the secondary roads. The countryside is ideal for leisurely touring and exploration. Good inns, good hotels, and good restaurants abound. Highways and roads are extremely well marked. You may take your own car to France, but it will be expensive to ship it over. Or you may rent a car, or buy one with a resell agreement. Your travel agent, the American Automobile Association, or the major U.S. car rental companies can help you make arrangements to rent a car in France before you leave. In France, arrangements can be made through the Automobile Club of France, 6 Place de la Concorde, Paris, or the C.S.N.C.R.A. (French Association of Self-Drive Agencies), 6 Rue Léonard de Vinci, Paris, or the S.N.C.F., 127 Avenue des Champs-Elysées or 16 Boulevard des Capucines, Paris. Under an S.N.C.F. plan, you can make your long hauls by train and they'll have a self-drive car waiting for you at your destination. The AAA can give you information on rules of the road in France, or ask the French Tourist Office for its brochure on motoring in France. Your valid American driver's license is sufficient, but you must have third-party insurance.

Who Can Help You Plan Your Trip? Your travel agent will charge you nothing for arranging transportation. For planning a detailed itinerary, securing hotel accommodations, etc., he will charge a small fee based on the complexity of your trip. For detailed information about various sections of France and about particular facets of travel, write to the French Government Tourist

Trained pigs are used to root out truffles, famed French delicacy, Southwest France.

Office nearest you. If you are a student, write to the Office du Tourisme Universitaire, 972 Fifth Avenue, New York, New York 10021, for the booklet describing a wide variety of special reduced-rate services available to you.

What Can You Read About France Before You Go? A list of good books about France would be almost endless. Here, however, are the titles of a *very* few that will provide some background and increase your enjoyment of your trip. You will find them at most libraries.

A History of France, by André Maurois. A lively and fascinating account, by no means ponderous.

Saint-Simon at Versailles, by Nancy Mitford. Story of the famous writer who chronicled the life of the French court of Louis XIV and Louis XV.

Queen of France, by André Castelot. Biography of Marie Antoinette, particularly colorful in describing the life of the court of Louis XVI and the coming of the French Revolution.

Journal of Eugène Delacroix (condensed version). Diary of the famous French painter who numbered among his friends and acquaintances most of the great names of his day—George Sand, Alexandre Dumas, Balzac, Baudelaire, Berlioz, Chopin, Liszt, Corot—who come vividly to life in his descriptions, as does Paris of the period from 1847 to 1863.

Shakespeare & Company, by Sylvia Beach. A description of literary and intellectual Paris in the 1920s and 1930s, by the woman whose bookstore (called Shakespeare & Company) was the focal point for much of its activity.

The Longest Day, by Cornelius J. Ryan. A description of the D-Day landing on Normandy beaches in World War II.

Bouquet de France, by Samuel Chamberlain. A massive gourmet tour of France, describing towns, naming restaurants, giving recipes, lavishly illustrated. Excellent, extremely detailed background for the pleasures of eating in France.

Cathedral of Notre Dame rises above roofs of Paris, France.

IN FRANCE

Wining and Dining. You will eat better in France than anywhere else in the world. In matters of cuisine, the French bow to no one. Only to the subtlest specialties of the Chinese do they even deign to nod.

French cooking is based on a subtle blend of tastes and textures, and depends largely on the extreme freshness of the ingredients (lack of refrigeration is a blessing, for there are no left-overs), the excellence of the meat and fish, and the delicacy of the sauces with which they are married.

To enjoy French cooking to the utmost, you should enjoy it as the French do. Since almost everything, everywhere, is cooked to order, you cannot expect to combine a good dinner with an evening on the town—unless you're willing to start your evening on the town about 11 p.m. If you wish to start earlier, take your main meal at mid-day, as the French often do. A round or two of martinis before a meal will kill your taste for the pleasures that follow. Choose an aperitif instead, or scotch and water. Order the *specialités* unless you're really allergic to them. They're not left-overs that the chef is trying to push, but the dishes that are his

Years of work in the sun line the face of this grape-harvester, Alsace, France.

proudest achievement. Any regional specialties (mentioned later
in sections on the provinces) are bound to be good. In Paris and
major restaurants of the Riviera, of course, you will find
specialties from everywhere.

A discussion of French cooking is best backed into, perhaps,
by explaining what it is not, for misconceptions abound. Though
many herbs and seasonings are used, it is not highly seasoned.
Only in specialties of the south of France will you find much
garlic and olive oil. It is not excessively rich, unless you persist in
ordering cream sauces. (There are plenty of others.) Though the
bread is delicious, starch is not considered a basic food, and you
may eat your way through France without ever seeing a potato or
a noodle, or missing either. Frying, and particularly deep frying,
are extremely rare. Meat, fish, and poultry are usually grilled,
broiled or baked—the Frenchman is far more conscious of his
insides than you are of yours. Though French pastry is world-
famous, cheese and fruit are much more favored as desserts. In
short, you need not worry about "adapting" to French cooking.
It is, on the whole, lighter, fresher, and more healthful than ours
—and a good deal tastier.

The only adapting you need do is about the matter of breakfast.
This is considered a very minor meal by the French—usually
consisting of bread or rolls (*croissants* are a favorite), honey or
jam, butter, coffee or tea. If you order juice, eggs, bacon, ham or
sausages, you will complicate both your breakfast and your bill.
The petit-déjeuner that is often included in your hotel bill is a
"continental breakfast" consisting of what the French call a *café*
or *thé complet*, with only the ingredients mentioned before,
usually served in your room. If breakfast is not included in your
bill, you may pare the cost a bit if you take it at a nearby café and
not in the hotel—ordering still only the *thé* or *café complet*. If
you're wild for fruit at breakfast, buy an orange or a tangerine at
the market the day before. No one will think it odd for you to
have a little stock of fruit in your room.

A French menu is worth a bit of discussion because it is often
written in an ornate, purple script that is rather hard to read, and
it is set up rather differently. French meals come in a series of
small courses, generally hors d'oeuvres first, then egg dishes

Moulin Rouge and Cyrano's, two famous night clubs, Pigalle, Paris, France.

(*oeufs*), soups (*soupes or potages*), main courses (*plats du jour*), vegetables, (*légumes*), cheeses (*fromages*), desserts and coffee. Usually salad will be on the menu too, and sometimes fish dishes (*poissons*). You don't have to order one of each—dinner usually consists of *hors d'oeuvres* and/or soup, a main dish from either *plats du jour* or *poissons,* a vegetable or a salad, cheese, perhaps a dessert, and coffee. When the menu says *couvert,* it means cover charge, sometimes figured as bread and butter charge instead. In general, *hors d'oeuvres* are a better bet than soup as your first course, because they can be far more varied. Among the most popular are artichokes (*artichaut*), snails (*escargots* with garlic butter), mussels (*moules*), *pâté* (a ground meat-loaf slice ranging from the hearty *pâté maison* to the delicate *pâté de foie gras,* but always delicious). If your main dish is called *garni,* a vegetable or two will come with it. If not, you must order a vegetable separately, or order a salad. When you see a vegetable with the adjective *primeur,* it means first of the season, and is bound to be a delicious treat. French cuts of beef may be confusing, but are excellent, and explained below. Kidneys, brains, liver, sweetbreads, are all splendid delicacies. Lamb may be cooked rather less than you are used to. The French like it still pink, as we like steak. Try it and you will see why.

There has been a great deal of to-do about which wine to order when, and why. Don't let it intimidate you. A basic rule is: red wine goes with red meat, white wine goes with poultry and fish. Beyond this, let the wine steward (*le sommelier,* with the chain around his neck) be your guide. Unless you are engaged in a grand dinner in a great restaurant, you need not order a different wine for each course. In fact, the table wine that comes in a carafe and is called *vin ordinaire* may suit you very well. In the more modest restaurants, you may ask for either red or white, and cut it with water, as the French do. Pink *rosé* wine is often a good compromise, though it will certainly cause the *sommeliers* in the great restaurants to wince. The only wine that may be served throughout an entire *luxe* meal is champagne, at a much steeper tariff, of course. Be consoled, however, by the fact that most French people these days order only one wine (and usually a *vin*

Beautiful hamlet is place where the Queen, Marie Antoinette, used to play at being a shepherdess, Versailles, France.

ordinaire) to see them through an entire meal. If you would prefer not to have wine, and are dining in one of the innumerable good but not great French restaurants, don't hesitate to insist on beer or bottled water. The French often do the same. Among the waters, *Evian* is still, *Vichy* is a bit carbonated, *Perrier* quite bubbly. Tap water, safe anywhere, though a request for it will horrify your waiter, is called *eau naturelle* or, facetiously, *Château la Pompe.*

The only other aspect of French cuisine that may require a bit of getting used to is French coffee, the famous *café filtre.* It takes forever for it to brew in that little inverted individual pot; you may burn your fingers in trying to nurse it into your cup; and the taste is both bitter and strong, but the memory of the taste of *café filtre* and of the fumes of a French cigarette may, long after you return, evoke your sharpest memories of France. You may, if you prefer, order *café américain* in many places, or tea *(thé)*. Order them after dinner, though. You may try to order them during, but you will rarely succeed. "Coffee with" and cereal are two things the French simply cannot comprehend. If you should feel yourself beset by a queasy stomach from too much excitement or too much travel, just order an omelette—which will be bland and splendid—and a *tilleul* or *infusion,* a French herb tea guaranteed to cure anything.

The outside appearance of a French restaurant does not necessarily correspond at all to the quality of its food. Some of the best restaurants are the least pretentious-looking. Definitely on your side, however, is the practice of posting the menu outside the restaurant, so you may browse through the specialties (and your pocketbook) at leisure before entering. Restaurants that do not post their menus outside are, generally, extremely expensive. On seeing the menu, you can figure your total bill, with wine and service, will come to about twice the price of the main dishes.

Noting the rising prices of French restaurants, the French government has instituted a system of *restaurants de tourisme,* under which cooperating restaurants offer daily fixed-menus ("tourist menu") including *hors d'oeuvre,* main course, cheese or dessert at regulated prices depending on the official category of the restaurant from $1.50 to $4.00. Wine and service are not included in these charges. Ask for the *menu touristique* if you'd like it; some restaurants produce it only on demand. You may,

View of St. Tropez harbor, Riviera resort made famous by French actress, Bridget Bardot.

however, get step-child service if you ride on the tourist menu in any of the luxury restaurants. Far better to go there with both open mind and open purse.

Don't turn up your nose at the *buffets de gare,* restaurants in the railroad stations. They frequently serve some of the best fare in France, particularly in the provinces, and at moderate prices.

In Paris and the larger cities, you will find cafeterias and self-service snack bars to patronize when your time and cash are limited. Not gourmet, certainly, but adequate. Look for signs that say "Libre Service," or ask the French Tourist Office for the booklet listing *Restaurants Self-Service.*

If you plan to be on your own in France, or to spend much time there, your best investment will be the *Guide Michelin,* which lists and rates a vast percentage of the country's restaurants. Its 3 star entries (meaning "extraordinary") are generally worth the trip in themselves. Michelin's famous separate "Green Guides" describe places of interest along the way. Some of them are published in English editions, notably Paris, Chateaux of the Loire, and the Riviera. If you're serious about sightseeing, they're invaluable.

When asking for your restaurant bill and contemplating your tip, see if service is included (if so, it's called *service compris*). In a middling restaurant, when service is included, you need not leave more than your small change. If the wine steward has helped you, however, you should tip him extra, usually 1 F at least, more in top restaurants. If service is not included, 12 to 15 per cent is the usual tip, 20 per cent in the very top places. Anywhere, *service compris* or not, it's considered gracious to leave your small change. Tip headwaiters only if they give you extra-special service in top restaurants. Tip bartenders 12 to 15 per cent if service is not included.

If it's just a snack you're after, your best bet is a café, not a restaurant. Most cafés will fix a sandwich for you—ham or cheese almost everywhere, sometimes something more elaborate. If you feel an overwhelming urge for a milkshake or a hot fudge sundae, you can find it at Le Drug Store. But the drug store on Main Street was never like this—they serve cocktails, too. Pam-Pam, near American Express, also does well by snacks, sandwiches and American breakfasts. But try the French way—it's superb.

Statue of Joan of Arc, at Orleans, France.

MENU TRANSLATOR

Viandes	Meats
boeuf	beef
biftek	steak

order *bein cuit* for well done, *à point* for medium rare, *bleu* or *saignant* for rare

boeuf bourguignon	beef stew in red wine sauce
châteaubriand	porterhouse steak
entrecôte	rib steak
contre-filet	sirloin steak
filet de boeuf	tenderloin
filet mignon, tournedos	center of filet
pot-au-feu	beef stew with vegetables
rosbif	roast beef
agneau	lamb
carré d'agneau	rib roast of lamb
côtelettes d'agneau	lamb chops
gigot	leg of lamb
poitrine d'agneau	breast of lamb
porc	pork
carré de porc	pork loin
charcuterie	pork cold cuts
cochon de lait	suckling pig
côtelettes de porc	pork chops
jambon	ham
veau	veal
blanquette de veau	veal stew
cervelle de veau	calf brains
côtes de veau	veal chops
escalope de veau	a slice from rib or filet
foie de veau	calf's liver
noix de veau	chunks from the rump
ris de veau	sweetbreads
rognons de veau	veal kidneys

Grimacing gargoyle atop Notre Dame Cathedral gazes out over Paris, France.

gibier	wild game
grenouille	frog
lapin	rabbit
mouton	mutton
saucisse, saucisson	sausage

Volaille — **Poultry**

canard	duck
caneton	duckling
coq	cock
dinde, dindonneau	turkey
faison	pheasant
oie	goose
pintade	guinea hen
poulet	chicken

Poisson — **Fish**

anguille	eel
crevettes	shrimp
ecrevisse	crayfish
escargots	snails
fruits de mer	mixed shellfish
homard	lobster
huîtres	oysters
langouste	rock lobster
maquereau	mackeral
moules	mussels
morue	cod
perche	bass
saumon	salmon
thon	tuna
truite	trout

Abats — **Insides**

cervelles	brains
foie	liver

Ornate hallway of Fontainebleau Palace once used by Napoleon, near Paris, France.

langue	tongue
rognon	kidney

Légumes — **Vegetables**

aubergine	eggplant
champignons	mushrooms
chou	cabbage
chou-fleur	cauliflower
cresson	watercress
épinards	spinach
flageolets	baby lima beans
haricots	beans
haricots verts	string beans
laitue	lettuce
oignon	onion
petits pois	peas
pommes de terre	potatoes
riz	rice

Divers — **Miscellaneous**

gâteau	cake
glace	ice cream
tarte	tart or pie
fromage	cheese
potage	soup (usually thick)
beurre	butter
pain	bread
lait	milk
café au lait, thé au lait	coffee with milk, tea with milk
sucre	sugar
oeuf	egg
oeuf dur	hardboiled egg
oeuf á la coque	boiled egg
oeuf sur le plat	fried egg
ail	garlic

Looking up through the trees at night, the Eiffel Tower appears to have been woven of spider webs or spun sugar, Paris, France.

NIGHTCLUBS AND MUSIC HALLS

You'll find plenty of nightclubs in Paris, of course, in other big cities, and in the major resorts. *Le striptease* is usually a major part of the show in nightclubs proper, although jazz, and occasionally folk singing, are features of the smoky Left Bank cellars, and the spiritually Left Bank cellars in other cities.

At nightclubs with shows, you can expect to pay a steep tariff. There is a minimum or cover charge which can range from 15 to 35 NF, and at most places the bottle of champagne at your table is obligatory and will cost you from $15 to $40. Whisky can cost you from $1.40 to $4.00 per drink, so stick to your champagne—you have to pay for it anyway.

Most famous of the Paris nightclubs is the Lido, with what many people consider by far the most spectacular floorshow. Others are the Crazy Horse Saloon, La Nouvelle Eve, Le Sexy, The Eiffel Tower and Olympia.

Tip: You can sample Paris night life least expensively on a "Paris By Night" tour, offered in several price ranges by hotels and travel agencies.

Jazz at the Living Room, gypsy music and Russian supper show at Sheherazade, Chez Raspoutine and Tzarevitch. Au Lapin Agile, for folk music and local color. New Jimmy's and Francois-Patrice's St. Hilaire, discotheques. Cellar nightclubs in the Latin Quarter include Chez Castel and Le Chat Oui Peche.

ACCOMMODATIONS

You will find all kinds of accommodations in France, from super de luxe to country inns, from modest *pensions* to motels. Everything for every taste and every pocketbook is here—but a few points bear keeping in mind.

Hotels
When the French say de luxe, they mean de luxe—in service, appointments, and price. If you'd aim for the Waldorf in New

Scattered throughout Paris, this Kiosk and others like it advertise theatrical events.

York or the Mark Hopkins in San Francisco, then you may want to aim for de luxe in France. Otherwise, aim at first class, or the simpler hotels. You'll pay less, and see more of the French way of life.

French hotels in all categories pride themselves on their service. You'll generally find everyone ready to help you and see to your comfort.

Are French hotels different? Yes, in some ways. Here's a rundown:

The greatest difference is that French hotels don't usually provide a bath with every room. Many of the grandest hotels, in fact, offer private baths with only about 60 per cent of their rooms. At the very same hotel, a room without bath can cost you from 30 to 50 per cent less than a room with bath. You always can take a bath, of course. Several rooms per floor are designated for the purpose. If you insist on a private bath, you'll usually get one, except in little places in the hinterland. But remember the steeper price you're paying. Unless you plan to spend half the day in the tub, you might better invest your travel money in an extra excursion, a fine dinner, a Paris dress.

In hotels below the luxury category, a private bathroom may turn out to be precisely that—with sink, tub, but no toilet, which, instead, will be down the hall. If the toilet is the apparatus you really want when you request a private bathroom, be sure that's what you're getting. It's common practice to ask to see your accommodations before you sign up for them. That's the time to count the pieces of plumbing equipment.

Some hotels require you to take your meals in. Fine if the hotel restaurant is where you want to eat; not so fine if the place down the block is world-famous. This practice is more frequent at heavily-booked spots such as resorts. Always check on it before you check in. The term to look for is *pension* or *demi-pension obligatoire*.

A real *pension* is the French version of a boarding house, usually much glorified. Guests must dine in, at least two meals a day. Though they come in all price ranges, *pensions* are generally smaller than hotels, and less impersonal. You may be able to

Chandeliers grace the grand staircase of the Opera House, Paris.

dicker for a lower rate than is first quoted. Generally, you will find *pensions* most enjoyable for a long stay in one place. They'll give you an opportunity to meet people, to feel at home. You pay one price for both room and board, there is no reduction in your rent if you eat out. If you're traveling on a budget in a resort area like, say, the Riviera, you may find a *pension* is exactly the answer to your needs. But if you're on a short trip, and intent on seeing all you can, a *pension* may cramp your style, because it limits your dining explorations.

Almost every French hotel of any size has on its staff a gentleman you'll want to get to know. He's the *concierge*—an intranslatable term combining bell captain, receptionist, money changer, ticket getter. In England, he's called the hall porter, but that designation really doesn't do him justice. When you want or need something, he's the man to see. He will hire a car for you, exchange your money, get you restaurant reservations, find you a doctor. You'll know him by the crossed keys he wears in his lapel, and by his look of harried elegance. He's a kind of super-liaison between management and staff. With him on your side, you're golden. (He has an equivalent, by the way, in Paris apartment buildings, also called the *concierge*, but likely to be an ample woman who acts as building superintendent and guardian of the gate, checking on arrivals and departures and overseeing the mail.) Tips to your hotel concierge are in addition to the hotel service charge. If he hasn't had to help you much and presents no extra bill, no tip is necessary. If he's been of average help in an average hotel, tip him 10 F per week. If he's helped you a great deal in an expensive hotel, tip him 30 F. If he's found you a dentist to pull your tooth on July 14, tip him more.

French hotels are categorized by the government in its system of "hôtels de tourisme." De luxe means that. Four stars means first class; three stars means very comfortable; two stars means second class; one star means third class. Prices are controlled only on three star hotels and lower. Four star and de luxe hotels are allowed to charge what the traffic will bear. A double room and bath in a four star hotel in Paris will run about $30 to $60. Luxury hotels cost more; lesser hotels less. Service charges—all

Looking down a typical street in Montmartre section, Paris, France.

those extras including taxes and tips—are not included in this fee, and usually run about 25 or 30 per cent more. Some hotels will quote an all-inclusive price called *prix forfaitaire*. Be sure you know whether the price mentioned is inclusive or not.

Hotel rates on the Riviera are about the same as in Paris, except that there are fewer middle-price hotels. Out in the country, apart from the famous resorts, you will pay less. You will also pay less off season.

For Paris and the Riviera, you should have your hotel reservations guaranteed before you leave the U.S. Elsewhere, if you are traveling leisurely and are not overly fussy, you may be happy with potluck. If your trip is a short one, however, on a tight schedule, pin down all your reservations before departure. Brittany, chateau country, Lourdes, can be fully booked months in advance. To avoid disappointment, it's always wise to have your reservations confirmed.

If you arrive in France without hotel reservations, an organization that will help you is the *Acceuil de France* (Welcome Information Office), with headquarters open daily from 9 a.m. to midnight. The Welcome Services can make reservations for you by teletype in the major cities of France. Provided, of course, accommodations are available.

If you're traveling on a budget, you'll want to know about *Les Logis de France,* which offer more than 1,600 economical hotels in pleasant surroundings, guaranteed to provide certain minimum standards at certain minimum rates. For the list of *logis,* write to the French Government Tourist Office nearest you.

Motels. This typically American invention is becoming more popular in France. At present you'll find motels in Antibes, Le Touquet, Villeneuve-Loubet-Plage, Mandelieu (near Cannes), Saint-Jean-de-Luz, Saintes-Maries-de-la-Mer, Aix-en-Provence, Marseille, Les Angles, Chonas (near Vienne), Rabot, Rocamadour, Tresseure, Houches, Saint-Aygulf, Bedarrides, and Pont de l'Isere. More are planned. Many have swimming pools, gardens and are air-conditioned.

Dawn breaks over garden of Cluny Museum, Paris, France.

Youth Hostels. Several hundred hostels in France are open to bearers of the Youth Hostel Federation Card. Overnight fee is minimal, but only the larger hostels rent sleeping bags, so it's wise to have your own equipment.

Student Accomodations. Write to the Office du Tourisme Universitaire, c/o French Cultural Service, 972 Fifth Avenue, New York, 10021, for information on the many student hostels and student restaurants.

COMMUNICATIONS

Mail service is very efficient, and is handled by the "PTT" (Poste, Télégraphe et Téléphone). You may buy stamps and the convenient air-letter forms at post offices, tobacco shops, or from your hotel concierge.

Telephones are dial-operated in most large cities. Pay phones can be found in post offices, railroad and subway stations, curbside booths, tobacco shops, restaurants and cafés. They take tokens, not coins, available at post offices for the official price, from the cashier at cafés and restaurants for a slightly higher price. Ask for a *jeton.* Insert it in the slot before you take down the receiver, dial your number, when you hear a voice at the other end, push the button marked "A." If you get no answer, hang up and push button "B" to get your token back. Long-distance and overseas calls may be made through the switchboard at your hotel.

WHAT'S GOING ON WHEN

Closing Times

Department Stores and specialty shops are usually closed on Sunday—open 9 a.m. to 6:30 p.m. Monday through Saturday.

One of Les Bouquinistes, or bookstalls, which line the Seine, Paris, France.

Many stores close in August. Stores also close on the following French national holidays:

January 1	July 14—Bastille Day
Easter Monday	August 15—Assumption Day
May 1—Labor Day	November 1—All Saints Day
Ascension Thursday	November 11—Armistice Day
Pentecost Monday	December 25—Christmas

Museums in Paris are usually open from 10 a.m. to 5 p.m. six days a week; closed on Tuesday and holidays. In other cities, hours are generally 10 a.m. to noon and 2 p.m. to 5 p.m.; closing day is usually Monday. Some museums in Paris are also open on Friday evenings, when galleries are illuminated.

Theatres close one day a week, but the day varies. Matinees are given at 3 p.m. on Sunday. Usually seats may not be purchased more than eight days in advance—so you have a good chance of getting a ticket for whatever you want to see, since performances are not sold out months ahead of time.

All the News

Newspapers and magazines are sold at kiosks. You'll find the International Herald Tribune which is published daily in Paris, as well as British and French papers. In Paris and other cities, you'll also find American newsmagazines.

Local amusements—movies, plays, concerts, lectures, sports events, exhibitions—in Paris are listed (partly in English) in the weekly magazine called *Une Semaine de Paris*, found at all newsstands. The National Office for Tourist Information, 127 Avenue des Champs-Elysées, provides a similar list in its free *Parisian Weekly Information*. Outside Paris, information on events and amusements is provided by the local Syndicats d'Initiative in cities and towns throughout the country. It's a good idea to make a beeline for the Syndicat office soon after you arrive in a town, to find out what's being offered while you're there.

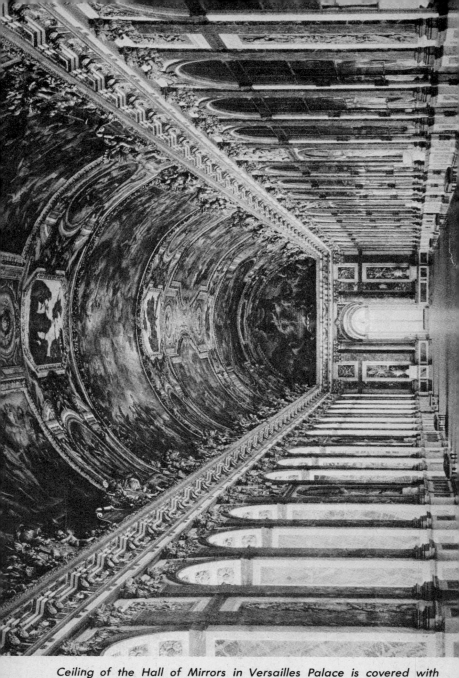

Ceiling of the Hall of Mirrors in Versailles Palace is covered with paintings by the Masters.

Tip: Major events to look for are the *Son et Lumíere Spectacles* (Sound and Light programs) in which chateaux and cathedrals are illuminated and sound effects evoke their histories.

In addition, many other chateaux and cathedrals are floodlit on summer evenings. Schedules vary widely, so check with your travel agent, tourist agencies in Paris, or local Syndicats outside Paris.

Ask your travel agent or the French Government Tourist Office for the annual list of events in France, which includes festivals, fairs, sports events, expositions.

SHOPPING
Browsing is a delightful pastime in France, and you're bound to end up buying most of the time. Just remember that you may bring into the U.S. only $100 worth of goods duty-free, and that you must somehow get your purchases back to the United States. You may take them in your luggage, but bear in mind your 44- or 66-pound air limitation, because excess-baggage charges are very expensive. If you have your articles shipped to you, you will have packing or crating charges, as well as transportation fees. There are also limitations on the amounts of certain kinds of articles that you may bring into the U.S. Liquor and perfume are among them.

While you are in France, you may, however, send to the U.S. small gifts that won't count against your $100 exemption if they are marked "Gift, value less than $10." You may not send perfume, liquor, or tobacco this way, and you may not send more than one package per day. Otherwise, you may send as many of these gift parcels as you like.

When making purchases, always get a receipt to confirm their value for customs purposes.

In many stores you may buy French goods at up to 30% discount on purchases. There is red tape involved, however. Refund checks are mailed to your home by the store, or you can obtain the refund upon turning in the documents to the Customs Official at a previously specified point of departure from France.

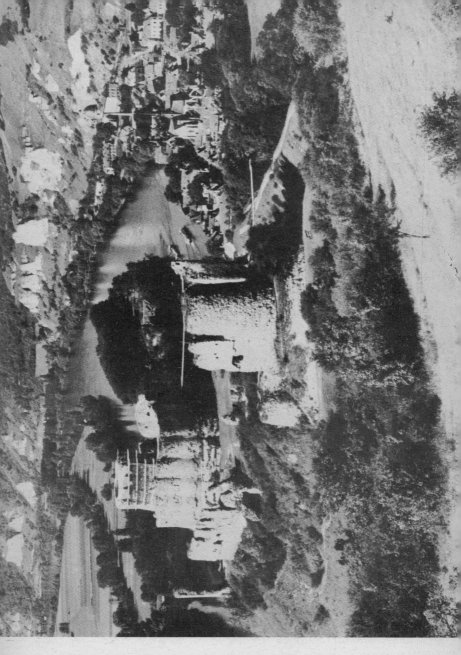

Almost totally in ruins, the Chateau Gaillard, home of Richard the Lion-Hearted, stands on a hill overlooking the Seine, Normandy, France.

What To Buy? Clothes are among the most famous products of France, of course. If you can afford them, clothes from the great fashion designers are the very finest and the very latest. Many designers also offer "boutique" collections of ready-to-wear clothes, and accessories at relatively modest prices. Other good buys are handmade lingerie, childrens' clothes, linens, blouses, gloves, handbags, scarves, shirts, ties, leather goods, umbrellas, hats, laces, handkerchiefs, china, crystal, porcelain. And, of course, perfume, vintage wines, liqueurs, champagne.

Tobacco. Several brands of American cigarettes are available in France, but are quite expensive. French cigarettes have a strong, distinctive, rather bitter flavor which may or may not be to your taste, but you'll never know unless you try them. Among the popular brands are *Gitanes, Gauloises* (the closest to American style). There is a charge for matches.

Stark and solid, the castle at Tarascon rises on the bank of the Rhone, Provence, France.

VISITING FRANCE

Paris and Environs. On an old map, Paris appears as a heart pierced by a river. Heart of this heart is Ile de la Cité, a tiny island in the Seine where Paris began as a village called Lutèce. Lutetia in Latin meant "marshland," which the spot was, and the name is perpetuated today in the Paris district called the Marais, also meaning marshland—a section of the Right Bank which was often flooded by the Seine.

Lutetia and its inhabitants, the Parisii, were mentioned by Caesar in his *Gallic Wars.* In times of peace, the city overflowed its island core, spreading to the right bank of the river and then to the left, to retreat again, in times of war, to the safety of the island. Over the centuries, new ramparts marked each era of the city's expansion. In 1845, the greatly enlarged city was enclosed for the last time by fortifications approximately outlining the limits of the city today. Within these bounds, by 1870, Baron Haussmann, under the appointment of Napoléon III, had pushed his great boulevards through the maze of medieval streets, creating modern Paris.

Town Square in picturesque village of Kayserberg, France.

Getting About. Paris is divided by nature into Right Bank and Left Bank, and by man into 20 *arrondissements* or wards. These useful designations, which often take their names from a prominent feature of the district—Louvre, Panthéon, Opéra—are the basis of the best maps of Paris, and a general knowledge of them helps make Paris a manageable city for the tourist.

Whether you wish to see Paris by guided tour, by taxi tour, by public transportation, or on foot, a *Plan de Paris Par Arrondissements* will be an invaluable asset in getting your bearings. On sale at all newsstands, this fat little book contains an individual map of each *arrondissement* showing every street, park and monument, an alphabetical directory to the streets, addresses of just about everything you'd want to find (including embassies, museums, theatres, post offices, libraries), and bus and subway maps. Next to your concierge, it's probably your best friend in Paris, and can save you from jumping into a taxi to get to a street that's just around the corner.

Subways. Once you catch on, the subway (called the *Métro*) is the fastest, cheapest, and easiest way to get about. Luckily, catching on is very easy. The Métro is so clearly marked that you can find your way without having to ask directions. At every entrance there is a large map, and at many stations there is also an electric route indicator to show you how to get where you want to go. Just push the button naming the station to which you want to go, and the shortest route will light up on the map. If you have to transfer to get to your destination, transfer points (called *correspondences*) are clearly marked. Lines are identified by the name of the terminal station. Tickets are sold at booths one flight down from street level. You can buy a single ticket or, at a reduced rate, a booklet of 10 tickets, called a *carnet*. There are first and second classes on the Metro. First class carriages are painted red. If you travel first class, hang on to your ticket even if it's on its second trip. An inspector can get on at any station and ask to punch it. An automatic gate will prevent you from dashing onto the platform when a train is approaching or in the station. Certain numbered seats are reserved for the blind, the disabled, for

Women do laundry in river under shadow of medieval castle, Josselin, France.

pregnant women and persons accompanying children under 4. If the car is crowded, you will be expected to give up your seat to someone in these categories. (Buses have these privileged seats also.)

Buses. Traveling by bus is rather more complicated, but much more scenic. Bus routes are designated by numbers. At bus stops are posts showing, on the street side, the name of the stop, and, on the sidewalk side, the route the bus takes from there to the terminal. The name of the terminal is marked on the front and rear of the bus, and on its side are listed the principal stops. At major bus stops, a little metal box dispenses numbered slips. Take one. It shows your place among the waiting passengers. When the bus comes, the conductor will call for *priorités,* and will admit first those carrying *cartes de priorité.* Then he'll call for *nombres,* and the rest of the waiting passengers will board in the order of their numbered slips, until the bus is full. You'll have to be pretty good at numbers to know when your turn comes. Buses don't stop unless someone is getting off or they are signalled, so always signal. You buy your ticket from the conductor. The route is divided into sections marked on the map in the bus. Each section costs one ticket. You may tell the conductor your destination and pay your single fare to that point, or you may buy a *carnet* of 10 tickets (less expensive), in which case the conductor will detach the necessary number of tickets representing the fare to your destination. After he punches your tickets, the conductor will return them to you. Hang on to them. As in the Métro, an inspector may come through, and if you've thrown your tickets on the floor or out the window, you may have to pay all over again. If you have a choice, sit by a window facing the map of the route, so you can figure out where you want to get off. Ring the bell in the middle of the bus or at the door to signal for a stop. Stops are generally called out, but watch for yours anyway.

Bargain: Reduced rate tourist tickets (*billets de tourisme*), valid for 7 days' unlimited use on both Métro and buses, are available from the R.A.T.P. offices at 53 bis Quai des Grands-Augustin, or Place de la Madeleine (on the right side of the church), and also at the French National Railroad offices in the U.S.

Tranquility of Chartres, with its famous cathedral, (at right) France.

Taxis. Supposedly there are thousands in Paris, but you may have a hard time finding even one when you need it. A taxi with its sign lighted is free, but at lunch and dinner time many will have black hoods over their meters, meaning the driver is returning to his garage and won't take you unless you happen to be going in his direction. If you have to catch a train, a curtain, or an important appointment, arrange with your concierge to have a taxi for you at a certain time. The usual tip is 15% of the fare. For trips outside Paris, ask the approximate price before you start out. You will be expected to pay at least part of the return fare, to get the cab back into the city limits. Return fares should be posted in the taxi. Ask to see them. When taxis are lined up at a stand, take the first one. You may hail a passing taxi, but not within 20 meters of a taxi stand. Beware of the large meterless cabs that wait in front of hotels and nightclubs. They are private cars, their rates are not regulated by law, and they can charge you whatever they please. If you do take one, make your price first.

Horsedrawn Carriages. The few surviving *fiacres* offer the most pleasant, leisurely, and expensive way to see the city. Rates are not fixed, so make a deal with the driver—generally 15 Francs per hour. *Fiacres* are usually found at the Rond-Point des Champs-Elysées, the Madeleine, the Opéra, the Tuileries, the Eiffel Tower, the Bois de Boulogne.

Car-hire. You can hire a car with chauffeur through your hotel, or from among the many lined up at various tourist centers throughout the city. Set the price with the driver, on either a time or trip basis. Information about hiring chauffeur-driven cars can be obtained from C.S.N.E.R.T., 48 Rue de la Bienfaisance, or from the Commission de Tourisme of the Automobile Club de France, 8 Place de la Concorde.

Self-drive Cars. They're widely available. However, traffic and parking problems are just as bad in Paris as they are in any large city anywhere—and may seem worse to a driver unfamiliar with the streets, the signs, the regulations, and the language. Driving through the French countryside can be a joy. Driving in Paris is

Medieval castle at Chinon is now in ruins after being ravaged for years by kings and warriors, France.

something else again. If you would relish the thought of driving in, say, Manhattan, then driving in Paris may be for you. If you insist on driving yourself around Paris, the following will assist you in your folly: C.S.N.C.R.A., 6 Rue Léonard de Vinci, will provide names and addresses of numerous car-hire firms; the Commission de Tourisme of the Automobile Club de France, 8 Place de la Concorde, can arrange for hire of French or American cars by members of foreign motor clubs.

Tip: It's against the law to honk a horn within the city limits except in dire emergency. Cars approaching blind corners after dark blink their lights — an unnerving experience, whether you're driver or simply passenger in a careening taxi.

What Should You See? There are a great many things in Paris that "should" be seen—enough to fill a lifetime. What you should see depends entirely on your tastes and interests. You will probably want to see some of the most famous monuments and buildings—Notre-Dame, the Eiffel Tower, the Louvre. Then, whether your inclinations lead you to the shops along Faubourg St. Honoré, to the bookstalls along the Seine, you will still be seeing Paris. The visitor who walks mile after mile in museums is no more virtuous than the visitor who sits hour after hour in cafés—nor is the reverse true. You can't see everything. No Parisian has seen everything. Let the knowledge of that fact free you from the obligation of trying to see too much. Get an over-all view, see a few things well, return to the places where you would like to spend some extra time. If you try to get to know something about a few places in Paris you will learn more than if you try to see a little of everything.

What *should* you see? For an over-all view, here is a Paris sampler—a brief guide to the major points of interest, from which to choose what appeals to you.

What To See and How to See It. There are many ways to discover Paris; by air from its vistas—from atop the Eiffel Tower, from the towers of Notre-Dame, from the dome of the Panthéon, from the Arc de Triomphe, from Sacré-Coeur; or by land and river through its views—from bus or boat tours, from the bridges.

Harbor of fishing village, Honfleur, is used by English and French as a yacht basin, Normandy, France.

The best way, undoubtedly, is through a combination—a vista to get the lay of the land, a tour or two to get your bearings, then your own private discovery on foot. In no other city is walking so rewarding, so enjoyable, or so easy. Paris is dotted with oases— parks and cafés where you may rest as frequently and as long as you like. Your table in a café costs the price of whatever you wish to order—an aperitif, a beer, a coffee, a tea, a lemonade— for which you may also sit as long as you like, to read a paper, write post cards, or simply enjoy the passing parade. The waiter wouldn't think of asking you to move on.

Sightseeing Tours—By Boat. The famous *Bateaux Mouches* make numerous daily trips on the Seine from April 1 to November 1, leaving from Pont d'Alma on the Right Bank. The new, smaller *Vedettes Paris-Tour Eiffel* sail from Pont d'Iéna on the Left Bank.

Sightseeing Tours—By Bus. Half-day tours of "Historic Paris" and "Modern Paris," and an evening's worth of "Paris By Night" are offered. The city-run R.A.T.P. Cityrama offers a jazzy, three-hour tour in glass-domed buses with tape-recorded commentary in eight languages.

> *Tip:* Among the most interesting of the regular city bus routes are numbers 95 (Opéra to St. Germain des Prés), 73 (Etoile to Hôtel de Ville), 63 (Trocadéro to Pont de Sully), 69 (Champ de Mars to Père-Lachaise), 47 (Châtelet to Quai Montebello). They can help you get your bearings very inexpensively, if you have your *billet de tourisme*.

The Paris you will want most to see lies roughly within these limits: Palais de Chaillot to the west, Sacré-Coeur to the north, Place de la Bastille to the east, Boulevard de Montparnasse to the south. The descriptions that follow are grouped by neighborhood, generally corresponding to the boundaries of arrondissements, and moving from west to east.

Peace pervades the harbor of vacation resort, Antibes, France.

LEFT BANK
Around the Palais-Bourbon—7th Arrondissement

The Eiffel Tower. At the north end of the Champ de Mars rises the peculiar structure that has become the symbol of Paris. Designed by the French engineer Gustave Eiffel for the Paris Exposition of 1889, it was greeted with cries of horror by the French who considered it an eyesore and talked for the next 20 years of tearing it down. Gradually, however, it came to be accepted as a fixture of the Parisian landscape. On a clear day, the panorama of Paris from its second platform is breath-taking. The panorama from the third platform is even more so, if you are fond of heights. In a strong wind, the tower sways only a little.

From the second platform, 377 feet above the Seine, it may help you to get your bearings if you remember that you are on the south—the Left—bank of the river, and that everything you see on the other side of the river is on the north—or Right—bank. With your map in hand, things will fall in place easily if you think of the city spread before you as the face of a clock. Due north across the Seine at 12 o'clock is the Arc de Triomphe at the Etoile. As you move clockwise around the platform, from 12 to 2 o'clock you face the 8th Arrondissement on the Right Bank, in it are the Champs-Elysées and the Madeleine. At 2 o'clock, just north of the river, is Place de la Concorde. Beyond it in the distance are the Opéra, Place Pigalle, Montmartre, Sacré-Coeur, At 2:30, just north of the river, are the Tuileries gardens, the Louvre, Palais Royal. At 3 o'clock are Ile de la Cité and Notre-Dame. At 4 o'clock, in the foreground, is Hôtel des Invalides, in the distance, the Panthéon. Between them lie the Latin Quarter, the Sorbonne, St. Germain des Prés. At 5 o'clock, across the Champ de Mars, is the Ecole Militaire. Beyond it, in the distance, is the modern UNESCO building. From 5 to 7 o'clock, to the south, is the Vaugirard district, of less interest to the visitor. At 7 o'clock you will see the Seine again. From 7 to 11 o'clock, beyond the Palais de Chaillot, lies the Bois de Boulogne.

Elevators take you to the first, second, and third platforms. The hardy may also walk as high as the second platform (674 steps).

In front of lone wind-mill vineyard workers harvest grape crop, Anjou, France.

UNESCO Building. Near the Eiffel Tower, this star-shaped building is well worth a tour, to see works by Picasso, Henry Moore, Calder.

Les Invalides. This massive complex of buildings and courtyards was commissioned by Louis XIV in 1670 as a home and hospital for disabled soldiers. It once housed as many as 7,000; now, only a handful. Under the dome of Les Invalides lies the tomb of Napoleon. Among the tombs nearby are those of his son, the King of Rome, and of Marshal Foch. Around the imposing Court of Honor is the Musée de l'Armée, the finest military museum in the world. An effective "Sound and Light" is presented in the courtyard from Easter to November.

Musée Rodin, Rue de Grenelle, Rue de Varenne. Just to the east of Les Invalides, at the corner of Boulevard des Invalides and Rue de Varenne, is the Rodin Museum, in a beautiful Regency-style mansion. Many of the sculptor's most famous works are here, including "The Thinker" and "The Kiss." Lovely gardens surround the museum. Rue de Varenne and the parallel street to the north, Rue de Grenelle, are lined with beautiful 18th-century houses, many occupied today by ministries and embassies. Talleyrand lived at 50 Rue de Varenne, where Napoleon, Josephine, and Mme de Staël were frequent visitors. Alfred de Musset lived at 59 Rue de Grenelle. This neighborhood is heart of the Faubourg St. Germain which was the city's most fashionable residential neighborhood during the early part of the 19th century.

Palais-Bourbon. Built between 1722 and 1728 for the Duchess of Bourbon, daughter of Louis XIV by his mistress Mme de Montespan, the palace is today the meeting place of the French National Assembly. The original building, low and gracious, resembled a Roman temple. Napoleon had the present imposing Greek façade erected in 1807, to harmonize with the Greek appearance of the Madeleine across the river. Along the Seine, immediately to the west of the Palais-Bourbon, is the Ministry of Foreign Affairs, often called simply the "Quai d'Orsay," after the Quai on which it stands.

Surrounded by a wall originally built to protect it from marauders is the village of Valence, French Riviera.

Around the Luxembourg Gardens—6th Arrondissement
The city's two great 20th-century artistic-bohemian-intellectual centers are in this neighborhood—Montparnasse to the south, and St. Germain des Prés to the north. This is the Paris of artists, writers, beards, cellar-clubs, jazz, folk songs, and, in the cafés, endless talk over endless cups of coffee. Although a good many famous schools are in the neighborhood—the Ecole des Beaux Arts, for one—this is not, strictly speaking, the "Latin Quarter." It is rather the home of the "free-lance" intellectuals and would-be intellectuals, less concerned with formal classes than with conversation.

Montparnasse. At the intersection of Boulevards Raspail and Montparnasse are the cafés that were the former haunts of Lenin, Trotsky, Modigliani, Picasso, Gide, as well as those disassociated Americans whom Gertrude Stein labeled the Lost Generation. Montparnasse was the bohemian center of Paris before World War I and between the wars. Hemingway and Fitzgerald knew it well. The famous cafés—La Coupole, Le Dôme, Le Select—are still heavily patronized, but since World War II the intellectual center of Paris has shifted north to St. Germain des Prés.

St. Germain des Prés. Around the intersection of Boulevard St. Germain and Rue de Rennes are the cafés Flore and Deux Magots, made famous as the meeting ground of the Existentialist writers led by Jean-Paul Sartre. Across the street is the Eglise St. Germain des Prés, the oldest church in Paris.

Oasis: Behind the church is the tiny Place de Furstenberg, one of the most charming squares in Paris, planted with magnolia trees and reminiscent of a bygone age. During the last years of his life, Eugène Delacroix had his studio at number 6. The studio may usually be visited and contains a small and worthwhile museum with many of the painter's sketches and notebooks.

Panoramic view shows Nice, capital of the Riviera.

The cafés, bookstores, antique shops and art galleries of St. Germain des Prés are particularly lively in the evening, from about 7 to 11 p.m. To the north, along Quai Malaquais and Quai de Conti, are some of the famous bookstalls, where you may, or may not, find a bargain. Quai Voltaire, to the west of Quai Malaquais, is one of the most charming streets along the Seine. Ingres and Baudelaire are among the famous artists and writers who lived here, the former at numbers 11 and 17, the latter at number 19.

Luxembourg Gardens. The Luxembourg palace and its gardens were created in 1615 for Marie de Medici, wife of Henry IV. During the Revolution, the palace was used as a prison. Today it is the home of the French Senate. Over the years, however, the beauty of the gardens has eclipsed the fame of the palace. This is a favorite spot for wheeling baby carriages, playing cards, sitting in the sun. Children sail boats in the basin, and under chestnut trees near the center of the gardens is a famous puppet theatre.

Around the Panthéon—5th Arrondissement

Boulevard St. Michel, which divides the 5th and 6th Arrondissements, is "Main Street" for the Paris student—his famous "Boul Mich." To the east lie the numerous colleges and buildings of the University of Paris. In the tangle of streets around them are the bookstores, bistros, small hotels and restaurants that serve as "campus" for the decidedly independent French student. This is the Latin Quarter, so-called because Latin was both official and unofficial language of the university until the Revolution. It was in this area, opposite the ancient island village of Lutèce on what is now Ile de la Cité, that the Roman conquerors built their own city with baths, a theatre, a temple, and an arena. The arena still exists, and Roman relics still turn up in the neighborhood.

Musée de Cluny. Housed in the beautiful Hôtel de Cluny is one of the world's finest collections of medieval art and artifacts, including the splendid "Unicorn Tapestries." The building also contains a handsome chapel. Ruins of the Roman thermal bath are adjacent.

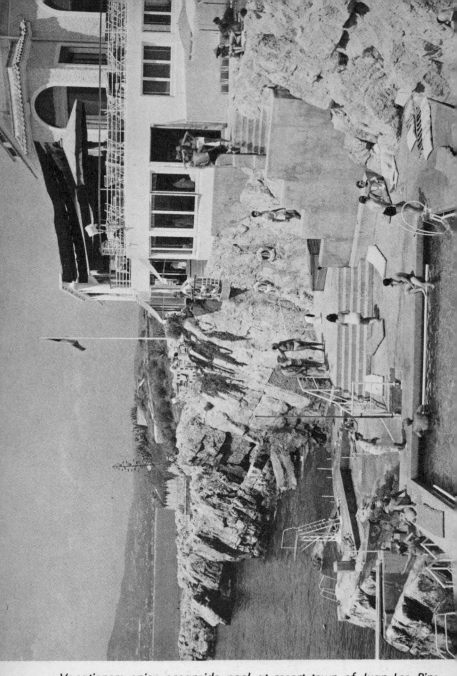

Vacationers enjoy oceanside pool at resort town of Juan Les Pins, Riviera, France.

The Sorbonne. This best known college of the University of Paris was founded in 1253 by Robert de Sorbon, chaplain to St. Louis. The present building dates mostly from the 19th century; the church, which contains the tomb of Cardinal Richelieu, from the 17th century. The huge building now houses part of the Faculty of Letters and Sciences, and the University library.

The Panthéon. Victor Hugo and Emile Zola are among the famous Frenchmen buried in this classic Temple of Fame. Built as a church in the latter part of the 18th century, it was consecrated as a mausoleum in 1791. Mirabeau, Voltaire, and Rousseau were the first three "great men of the epoch of French liberty" to be buried here. Anti-monarchists later had second thoughts about Mirabeau, and replaced his body with that of Marat, which was also eventually removed. There is a splendid view of Paris from the dome (425 steps).

Arena of Lutèce. The remains of the Roman arena lie several blocks to the east of the Panthéon. Built in the 2nd century, it held some 16,000 spectators at gladiatorial combats, exhibitions of wild animals, and other Roman pastimes. Destroyed toward the end of the 3rd century, it was slowly obliterated and forgotten, until rediscovery in 1869.

> *Oasis:* At the north of the district, between Boulevard St. Germain and the Seine, is the ancient quarter of St. Séverin, a maze of alleys and old houses that still give some idea of the Paris of the Middle Ages. Particularly interesting streets are Rue de la Huchette, Rue de la Harpe, and Rue du Chat qui Pêche, famous as the shortest street in Paris. From the little park at Square René Viviani, just behind the Church of St. Julien le Pauvre, there is a beautiful view of Ile de la Cité and Notre-Dame.

THE ISLANDS IN THE SEINE

The Heart of Paris—1st and 4th Arrondissements
Ile de la Cité was the site of the ancient village of Lutèce from

View of the quiet river, Gironde, which passes through Bordeaux, France.

which Paris grew. At one time it contained the residence of the king, the parliament, the university, as well as the cathedral. Today it holds the two finest Gothic monuments in Paris—Notre-Dame and Sainte-Chapelle. Both Sainte-Chapelle and the Conciergerie, infamous prison of the Revolution, are within the vast complex of turreted buildings that is now the Palais de Justice. Among the many bridges that link the Ile with the Left and Right banks, the most beautiful is the one at the western tip of the island, the Pont Neuf or "new bridge," which is, perversely, the oldest. On the island, too, are a flower market, many administrative buildings, several ancient streets, and two small and lovely parks.

Palais de Justice. The law courts occupy the mass of buildings that dominate the western end of the island, but you may visit two important sites within the walls. You must not miss the glorious 13th-century Sainte-Chapelle, with its magnificent soaring stained glass windows, and the grim cells and prisoners' gallery of the Conciergerie, where Marie Antoinette and hundreds of other condemned persons awaited their journeys to the guillotine.

Notre-Dame. Begun in 1163 and completed in 1345, this national church of France grew with Gothic Paris. It is the last of the great galleried churches, and the first with flying buttresses. From the twin towers are splendid views—beyond the heads of the gargoyles—over the city (387 steps). From these towers, bells were rung by Quasimodo, the Hunchback of Notre-Dame, in Victor Hugo's famous novel. Although the kings of France were traditionally crowned at Reims, they often came here for *te deum* celebrations. Napoleon was crowned here in 1804. Revolutionary mobs vandalized the church which was in crumbling disrepair by 1840. From 1844 to 1864, restorations were made by Viollet-le-Duc. The cathedral appears today much as it did in the 14th century.

Delicate architecture of Amboise Castle rises behind modern lines of bridge spanning Loire river, France.

Oases: At each end of the island are delightful parks. At the west is the Square du Vert-Galant; at the east, behind Notre-Dame, the Square de l'Archevêché.

One of the most beautiful and tranquil oases in all Paris lies just east of Ile de la Cité. It is the "other island," Ile St. Louis, reached by a footbridge. The charm and peace of 17th and 18th century Paris are preserved almost entirely intact. To savor them, you should visit the island on foot. It is very small.

RIGHT BANK

Passy—16th Arrondissement
Between the Bois de Boulogne and the Seine is one of the most fashionable residential districts of present-day Paris, a neighborhood of broad avenues and modern apartment buildings.

Palais de Chaillot. This huge building was built for the 1937 Exhibition; from its terraced gardens there are spectacular views across the Seine to the Eiffel Tower and the Champ de Mars. On this site a mansion was built for Catherine de Medici, and, later, the Palais de Trocadéro built for the 1878 Exhibition. The broad wings of the present Palais house a theatre and four museums. Musée de l'Homme is one of the world's finest anthropological museums. Musée de la Marine is probably the world's greatest museum of maritime history. The Musée des Arts et Traditions Populaires contains exhibits of French folklore.

Museum of Modern Art. One of the great museums of Paris, it contains a rich display of 20th-century painting and sculpture by such artists as Bonnard, Utrillo, Matisse, Picasso. In addition to the permanent collections, there are special temporary exhibits.

Around the Champs-Elysées—8th Arrondissement
Between Place Charles de Gaulle-Etoile and Place de la Concorde lies one of the great tourist centers of Paris, and one of the favorite centers of Parisians, too. Its main thoroughfare is the world-famous Champs-Elysées, the splendid avenue that sweeps

Ancient bridge, Cahors Pont Valentré, and modern village in background show the blending of past and present in France.

from Place de la Concorde to the Arc de Triomphe at the Etoile. Green and parklike to the Rond-Point, it becomes—even more than a street—a vast sidewalk lined with cafés, shops, movie theatres, nightclubs. On side streets are the showrooms of the *haute couture*—the great fashion houses of Dior, Chanel, Balmain, Balenciaga. The parallel street to the north is Rue du Faubourg-St-Honoré, one of *the* shopping streets in Paris, whether you care to buy or simply windowshop.

Arc de Triomphe. This massive arch was commissioned by Napoleon to honor his victorious armies, and begun in 1806. Today it has become the symbol of French national honor. On November 11, 1920, France's Unknown Soldier was buried here. A perpetual flame of remembrance burns above his tomb. Among the sculpture on the arch is the famous "Marseillaise" group by Rude, showing the goddess of war calling Frenchmen to defend their nation. From the platform atop the arch (272 steps, also an elevator), the plan of the Etoile becomes clear: it is called the star because from it radiate 12 broad avenues. Crossing the Etoile to reach the arch is, by the way, one the tourist's major occupational hazards. There is now an underground passageway for the cowardly.

The Champs-Elysées. In 1616, a series of tree-lined walks were laid out here for Marie de Medici. These shady avenues, called Cours-la-Reine, were the beginnings of today's Champs-Elysées, Paris' Elysian Fields. The avenue is the city's triumphal way, as well as one of the best places for café-sitting, whether you pick the greenery and fountains of a restaurant at the Rond-Point, or the bustle and asphalt of the upper avenue. There's a famous open air postage stamp market close to the Rond-Point, held Thursdays and Sundays.

Oasis: To the north of this district, in an elegant residential area, lies the equally elegant Parc Monceau. Far smaller than the Luxembourg or Tuileries gardens, its charm more than compensates for its lack of size. Within its shady bounds are ivy-covered colonnades, a pond, a Renaissance arcade.

Fishermen dot the river and its banks in picturesque Moselle, Northeastern France.

Place de la Concorde. One of the largest and most beautiful squares in the world, its fountains, colonnades and splendid vistas give little indication of its bloody history. It was commissioned in 1757 by Louis XV, whose statue decorated the center of the square until it was pulled down by rioting mobs in 1792, and the name of the square changed from Place Louis XV to Place de la Révolution. Heads fell there as well as statues. Louis XVI was guillotined there on January 21, 1793; among the 1,300 persons executed during the next two years were Marie Antoinette, Mme du Barry, Charlotte Corday, Danton, Robespierre. In 1795, the scaffold was finally removed, and the square renamed Place de la Concorde. The obelisk of Luxor, from the temple of Rameses II at Thebes, was raised in 1836. The view from the base of the obelisk toward the Champs-Elysées is one of the most magnificent in Paris. Reaching the obelisk through the swirling traffic is, however, a perilous project recommended only to the fleet-of-foot. The two imposing buildings at the north of the square are Ministère de la Marine (the navy) at the right, Hôtel Crillon at the left. Immediately to the left of the latter is the American Embassy, which harmonizes graciously with its surroundings.

Around the Louvre—1st Arrondissement

The streets just north of the Seine, between Place de la Concorde and Boulevard de Sébastopol, harbor some of the most splendid treasures of France, whether your criterion is esthetic or gastronomic. You may view the *Mona Lisa,* have a drink at the Ritz Bar, see a performance at the Comédie Française. The morning after, you may even find some peace and quiet in the gardens of the Palais-Royal as you contemplate an assault on the Bank of France, across the street, to refinance your trip.

The Tuileries. This 60-acre garden in the heart of the city is probably the most famous of the Paris parks. Here in the sun lovers come to hold hands and children come to watch puppet shows and sail their boats in the basins. The plan of the gardens was drawn up in 1563 for Catherine de Medici, and they retain their formal air in precise paths, symmetrical flower beds dotted

Bathers bask in the sun at the Atlantic resort of Biarritz, Basque country, France.

with statues, and wide avenues of chestnut and lime trees. If you sit in no other Paris park, you must sit, for a while at least, here. The Tuileries has known much violent history. Louis XVI and Marie Antoinette fled across its paths to seek asylum with the National Assembly. After receiving the cease-fire order from the king, their loyal Swiss Guard also tried to escape across the park, only to be slaughtered. In August 1944, the park was the scene of a bitter battle between tanks of the Leclerc Division and German troops dug in in the garden. At the west corners of the park are two museums, the Orangerie and the Jeu de Paume.

The Orangerie. See Monet's murals, "Les Nympheas," delicate paintings of waterlilies that are world-famous.

Jeu de Paume. Built in 1851 as an indoor tennis court, it contains the Impressionist collection of the Louvre. After the Louvre, it is probably the most important art museum in Paris. Among its masterpieces are works by Monet, Manet, Pissarro, Toulouse-Lautrec, Renoir, Gaugin, Van Gogh, Cezanne.

The Louvre. Most famous today as one of the world's great museums, the Louvre is first of all a palace, perhaps *the* palace of France. In the 12th century, Philippe-Auguste built a wall and tower here to protect the island-city. From that time, the complex of buildings grew almost continuously, occasionally—but by no means always—as residence of the king. Charles V enlarged the complex, turning it from fortress into royal residence. In the 15th century, the kings of France preferred to live in their chateaux on the banks of the Loire, or in other Paris palaces such as Hôtel des Tournelles near Place des Vosges. The 16th century saw a royal return to the Louvre, however, accompanied by remodelings and enlargements. Louis XIV lived at the Louvre until 1680, when he officially moved the court to Versailles. During the next 70 years, all sorts of people camped in the galleries—artists, pickpockets. By 1750 the Louvre was in such bad state there was talk of tearing it down. Marie Antoinette and Louis XVI stayed here briefly and uncomfortably during the tense days preceding the Revolution, but it was Napoleon I who finally drove out the

Picturesque peasant village of Annot, one of many found throughout Southern France.

squatters and began the work of restoring the palace, finished under Napoleon III. The Louvre today houses many of the great art treasures of the world. Among its most famous sculptures are the Venus de Milo and the Winged Victory of Samothrace. Among its most famous paintings are the *Mona Lisa*, Raphael's *Madonna*, Franz Hals' *Gypsy Girl*, Vermeer's *The Lace Maker*, Ingres' *Odalisque,* Millet's *The Angelus.* On Friday evenings throughout the year, various sculpture galleries of the Louvre are specially flood-lighted.

> *Tip:* Among portraits that may increase your enjoyment of French history are Clouet's and Titian's of Francis I, Rigaud's of Louis XIV, David's of Mme Recamier and of the Coronation of Napoleon, Prudhon's of Empress Josephine, Champaigne's of Cardinal Richelieu. The School of Fontainebleau painting of *Diana the Huntress* is thought to portray Diane de Poitiers, mistress of Henry II.

There are miles and miles of galleries in the Louvre. Wear your walking shoes, buy a guidebook in the lobby and try not to go on Sunday, when admission is free and the galleries are thronged. You may take pictures with a hand camera, but special permission is required to use a tripod.

Shopping Streets. Rue St. Honoré is one of the world's most elegant shopping streets. Place Vendôme and Rue de Rivoli are worth the shoppers' attention, too.

Palais-Royal. Built by Cardinal Richelieu in 1635 at his palace, it was subsequently the home of Louis XIII and Louix XIV. In the 18th century houses and shops were built around its gardens. It became the favorite walk of Parisians. It was also the scene of many famous and infamous parties, and became the site of gambling halls. It was also a meeting place for revolutionaries—at number 177, Charlotte Corday bought the knife with which she stabbed Marat. The gardens outside the Palais-Royal are charming. The building today is used as an administrative court.

A kiss ends this dance at Roussillon, Southwest France.

Around the Hôtel de Ville—4th Arrondissement
Between Boulevard de Sébastopol and Place de la Bastille lies the
ancient quarter of the Marais, heart of the Paris of the 17th
century. Its splendid 16th, 17th, and 18th century houses have
become tenements and shops, but some are being restored and
the district is well worth a visit.

Hôtel de Ville. The "City Hall" of Paris is at a spot often called the
cradle of revolution, rich in history and violence. The original
building, begun in 1553, was the scene of magnificent celebrations
and a great many executions. For a time during the Revolution,
the guillotine stood here. Eleven years after the old building was
burned by the Commune in 1871, the present building, a good
likeness, was inaugurated. In August 1944 when the Hôtel de
Ville was headquarters of the Resistance, there was heavy street
fighting in the neighborhood.

Musée Carnavalet. This museum dedicated to the history of Paris
is located in one of the city's most beautiful 16th century houses.
Here Mme de Sévigné lived for 20 years and wrote her remarkable letters.

Place des Vosges. The oldest square in Paris to retain its
appearance almost intact, Place des Vosges, a bit removed from
the usual tourist paths, is too often neglected. It was the site of
Hôtel de Tournelle, royal residence of Louis XII and Henry II,
whose queen, Catherine de Medici, had the building torn down
after he was killed in a tournament at Rue St-Antoine nearby. The
square you see today was built by Henry IV in 1605, beginning
with two large royal pavilions. Nobles of his court followed suit,
completely closing the square. Place Royale, as it was called
then, was inaugurated in 1612 with a gigantic festival which
included a parade with 1,000 horsemen. Soon the square became
the center of 17th-century Paris, so famous that it was simply
called "la Place." Under Louis XIII and Louis XIV it continued
to be a fashionable address. Richelieu lived at number 21. Though
eclipsed by Faubourg St-Germain in the 18th century, the square

Small craft crowd harbor at English resort of Menton, near Italian border, Riviera, France.

continued to draw residents whose names are remembered today. One was Victor Hugo, who lived at number 6, now the Victor Hugo Museum.

Place de la Bastille. No other name in Paris is so reminiscent of the Revolution. If the Hôtel de Ville was its cradle, Place de la Bastille was its birthplace. The site of the Bastille, built in 1370 as a fortress, but infamous thereafter as a prison, is marked by a line of white paving stones. Most of its prisoners—like the Man in the Iron Mask—were gentlemen who had somehow offended the Court and were condemned by royal decree rather than due process of law. Often they enjoyed semi-liberty and were even able to entertain their friends. The Bastille was a symbol of the abuses of the monarchy and the nobility and was stormed by angry mobs on July 14, 1789. Razing of the building began the next day. The guillotine erected here took more than 1,000 lives. Place de la Bastille is today part of a bustling working-class neighborhood, often the scene of Communist rallies on May Day.

Around the Opéra—9th Arrondissement, 2nd Arrondissement
This is the business-like center of present-day Paris, the Paris of shops, department stores, the stock exchange, the great boulevards. And, for the visitor, the Paris of Rue de la Paix, American Express, Cook's, and Café de la Paix (just across the street from the Opéra) where it's said you will, if you sit long enough, eventually see everyone you know.

The Madeleine. Reminiscent of a Greek temple, the Madeleine is one of the most fashionable churches in Paris. Begun in 1764 under Louis XV, its construction continued by fits and starts for almost 80 years, during which it was proposed for use as a library, legislative palace, railroad station, stock exchange, and national bank. Napoleon contributed the idea that it be completed as a temple of glory dedicated to the soldiers of his army, but decided on erecting the Arc de Triomphe for this purpose instead. In 1842, the Madeleine was opened as a church, its original purpose.

Tourist looks at lace being sold by lace-maker, Brittany, France.

The Opéra. Immense, lavish and ornate, the opera building devotes almost as much space to the pleasures of intermission as to the pleasures of the performance. Its Grand Staircase and Great Foyers seem to be extraordinary stage settings themselves. The Opéra ceiling, painted by Chagall in 1964, is an added effect to be enjoyed.

The Grand Boulevards. Many of the great streets of Paris were created between 1855 and 1870 by Baron Haussmann, Prefect of the Seine. Among them are Boulevard Haussmann, Boulevard de la Madeleine, Boulevard des Capucines, Boulevard des Italiens, Avenue de l'Opéra. Along them you will find the city's great department stores, specialty shops, theatres. This is the Paris of the businessman, a good place to get an idea of Parisian commercial activity. Traffic is heavy, streets are crowded, parks are few and far between, but cafés are plentiful.

Around Pigalle—9th Arrondissement, 18th Arrondissement
Where Boulevard de Clichy separates the 9th and 19th Arrondissements, "gay Paree" begins, demonstrating a decidedly split personality. To the north, around Sacré-Coeur, was the 19th-century Paris of the cancan and Moulin de la Galette—the Montmartre immortalized by Toulouse-Lautrec and Utrillo. To the south is Place Pigalle, a honky-tonk area of strip-tease shows, nightclubs, all-night movies, penny arcades. You may still see the cancan at one of the café-dance halls in Montmartre, or find an artist diligently painting one of the steep, twisting streets. But 20th-century commercialism has invaded Montmartre, and it has conquered Pigalle.

Place Pigalle. In this most feverish center of Paris night life, you will find practically any form of entertainment imaginable, or it will find you. Pigalle is a sad and shabby neighborhood by day, gaudy with neon by night. Most of your fellow visitors, you will notice, do not speak French. Known as "Pig Alley" during World War II, it still specializes in nude shows that aim to shock the tourist.

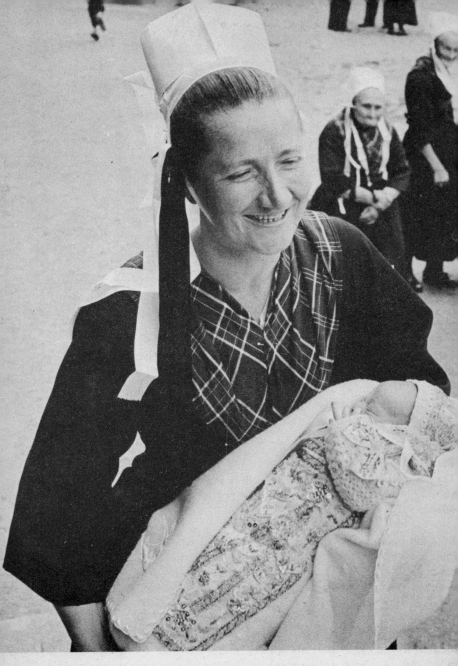

In traditional garb, mother carries her infant to christening, Brittany, France.

Tip: Tours of "Paris By Night," offered by the major tourist agencies, provide the least expensive way to see Pigalle, and other night spots.

Montmartre. During the late 19th century, Montmartre was the bohemian and artistic center of Paris. Renoir, Manet, Degas, Toulouse-Lautrec lived and worked in this neighborhood of winding streets and narrow staircases. The origin of the word "Montmartre" is ambiguous. It either stems from Hill of Martyrs, the spot where St. Denis was beheaded, or from Mons Mercurii, Hill of Mercury, site of a pagan temple. The ambiguity is perpetuated today in the nature of the neighborhood, once the romantic setting of the city's *vie de bohème,* still picturesque, but now a bit tawdry. Place du Tertre is its center, a square filled with outdoor cafés and lined with small restaurants. Crowning Montmartre, on the highest hill above Paris, is the famous Basilica of Sacré-Coeur. This enormous white church, begun in 1876, was built by public subscription as an act of atonement and of hope after the defeat of France by Germany. Like the Eiffel Tower, it draws mixed reaction from Parisians. From the dome of the church, or from the broad terrace in front of it, you may look down on the finest view of Paris—and decide for yourself what in Paris you "should" see.

THE FRINGES AND THE DEPTHS

The city's two enormous parks, its most famous market, and its subterranean curiosities make interesting short excursions—of widely varying appeal.

Bois de Boulogne. At the western side of Paris, bordering on Passy, is the city's most fashionable great-outdoors. Much of the huge park is a forest, with riding paths. There are also playgrounds, lakes, restaurants, and two world-famous race tracks—Longchamp and Auteuil.

Bois de Vincennes. This second of the great parks of Paris is located at the city's eastern fringe, next to the 12th Arrondissement. Again, there are forests, a race track. Of most interest,

Fishermen unload the day's "catch," Concarneau, Brittany, France.

however, is the magnificent Château of Vincennes, palace of the kings of France during the Middle Ages. Expanded, modified, rebuilt over a period of eight centuries, it preserves much from the 14th century, when Charles V undertook major improvements and made the chateau his favorite residence. In an ironic footnote to history, it was here that England's King Henry V died from an attack of dysentery, on the eve of an alliance with Burgundy. Around the castle is a famous zoo.

The Flea Market. The fascinating Marché aux Puces, named for the dividends offered in its second-hand bedding, is on the northern edge of the city, above the 18th Arrondissement. Take the Métro to Porte de Clignancourt, then walk north along Avenue Porte de Clignancourt. The majority of the shops and stalls are in the triangular area between Boulevard Périphérique and Avenue Michelet. Every imaginable kind of second-hand merchandise is available—and if you have a shrewd eye, you may be able to spot a bargain antique amid the piles of junk. Market days are Saturday, Sunday, and Monday.

The Catacombs. The underground limestone quarries dug by the Romans house millions of skeletons transferred from overcrowded cemeteries during the 18th and 19th centuries. From 2 Place Denfert-Rochereau (14th Arrondissement), guided tours leave at 2 p.m. every Saturday between July 1 and October 15; the rest of the year, on the first and third Saturdays of the month only. The section of the Catacombs just below the building where the tour starts was used as a headquarters of the French Underground movement during World War II.

The Sewers. These legendary escape-routes and hide-outs for Parisian criminals are actually relatively clean. You may think you see the Phantom of the Opera or Jean Valjean lurking in the shadows, as you sail along the tunnel from Concorde to the Madeleine. Guided tours leave from the statue of Lille at Place de la Concorde from 2 to 5 p.m. every Thursday from July to October 15. Check days and times for tours during the rest of the year.

Elaborate lace and embroidery decorate the lavish outfit of this youn[g] miss from Brittany, France.

HOTELS

You'll find a wide selection of hotels in every section of Paris, but to make the most of your time there, you'll probably want to stay in or near the section that interests you most. If broad streets, new shops, elegant restaurants appeal to you, a hotel on the Right Bank may be most convenient. Major hotel centers here are in the 1st Arrondissement, around the Louvre; the 2nd Arrondissement, around the Bourse; 8th Arrondissement, around the Champs-Elysées; 9th Arrondissement, around the Opéra. If the Latin Quarter and a look at *la vie de bohème* appeal to you, a hotel on the Left Bank may be your choice—in the 5th Arrondissement, near the Panthéon, or the 6th Arrondissement, near the Luxembourg Gardens. The most famous luxury hotels are on the Right Bank, but if you stay on the Left Bank you don't have to participate in bohemian existence unless you want to. There are plenty of excellent hotels on the Left Bank too.

In the following list, classification is noted by the letter or number in parentheses following the name of the hotel. L means luxury, 4 first class, 3 very comfortable, 2 second class.

RIGHT BANK

1st Arrondissement, near the Louvre
Inter-Continental (L); Meurice (L), Ritz (L), Louvre (4), Normandy (4), Mont-Thabor (3).

2nd Arrondissement, near the Bouse and Rue de la Paix
Westminster (4), Edouard VII (4), Dounou (3), Favart (2).

8th Arrondissement, near the Champs-Elysées
George V (L), Crillon (L), Plaza-Athenée (L), Prince de Galles (L), Bristol (L), Lancaster (L), California (4), Claridge (4), Napoléon (4), Elysées (3), Vignon (3), Maréchaux (2).

9th Arrondissement, near the Opéra
Le Grand Hotel (L), Ambassador (4), Commodore (4), Scribe (4), Florence (3), Victor Masse (2).

Traditional folk-dance performed at festivals in Grenoble, Brittany, France.

17th Arrondissement
Medien (L).

LEFT BANK

5th Arrondissement, near the Panthéon
Colbert (3), Albe (2), Mt. Blanc (2).

6th Arrondissement, near the Luxembourg Gardens
Lutétia (4), Victoria Palace (3), Pas-de-Calais (3), Hotel Nice and
Beaux Arts (3), St. Sulpice (3).

14th Arrondissement
St. Jacques (L).

15th Arrondissement
Paris Hilton (L).

RESTAURANTS

Paris has thousands of restaurants offering excellent meals in a
variety of price ranges. If cost is your main concern, remember
that if the menu is not posted outside, the restaurant is probably
very expensive. An evening at one of the most famous restaurants of Paris can run as high as $50 per person or more, but
hundreds of restaurants provide magnificent dinners for $5 or $6
per person, and thousands of restaurants provide excellent
dinners for less.

Among the most famous and expensive restaurants in Paris
are La Tour d'Argent, Maxim's, Lasserre, Allard, Ledoyen,
Taillevent, Roger Lamazere, Le Vivarois, Meurice and Laper-
ouse. Other justly renowned temples of gastronomy are Lucas-
Carton, Prunier's, Chez Garin and Chez Allard. Many top hotels
have excellent dining rooms: George V, Plaza Athenée, Ritz and
Paris Hilton.

Some medium price range restaurants you might try are
Fouquets, Auberge du Vert-Galant and Marius et Janette.

Three widows, their men lost at sea, descend from chapel, Brittany, France.

There are U.S. snack-type places, le self-service cafeterias and charcuteries (sort of delicatessen) for simple or sophisticated do-it-yourself picnic fare to eat in the park. Paris has wonderful restaurants specializing in foreign cuisine of every country.

Tip: Many restaurants close one or two days a week, and some close during July or August. Always check to be sure a restaurant is open before making a special trip to it. In the more expensive restaurants, always make a reservation.

AROUND PARIS

The ring of woods and valleys surrounding Paris is dotted with chateaux, fortresses, and cathedrals almost as prodigally as it is with poplars, beeches, and willows. This is the Ile de France, the heart of France, participant in 2000 years of French history and custodian of its splendors. Here are the royal palaces of Versailles and Fontainebleau, the cathedral of Chartres, the forests and villages immortalized by the painters Corot, Pissarro, Cézanne, Monet, Sisley. Not far away are Château-Thierry and Belleau Wood. Historically and architecturally, Ile de France is France in miniature—none of it more than a half-day's drive from Paris.

The major tourist agencies operate half-day and all-day guided bus tours to the points of interest. Fast local trains and buses also go to Fontainebleau, Versailles, and Chartres, as well as to the rest of the region. Probably the best way to see Ile de France, however, is by car.

During the summer, *Son et Lumière* spectacles are frequently presented at the major monuments, including Chartres, Versailles, and Compiègne. Check dates and times.

Tip: It is possible—*but just humanly possible*—to visit both Versailles and Chartres in the same day. However, these are two of the most spectacular sights in France. If you try to cram them both into one day, you'll be cheating yourself.

Young women are serenaded by bagpipes, Nantes, France.

SOUTHWEST OF PARIS

Versailles. The immensity of the main palace and its gardens must be seen to be believed. And they are not all Versailles. You will want also to see the two Trianon palaces, and Marie Antoinette's make-believe village. Versailles is royal France at its pinnacle, and remains eloquent testimony to the reasons for both its glory and its fall. At the time of Louis XIII, Versailles was a royal hunting lodge and nothing more. The vast palaces and gardens were commissioned by Louis XIV. Distrustful of Paris, wishing to keep a close eye on his nobles, above all outraged by the palace built at Vaux-le-Vicomte by his own finance minister, he commandeered the latter's architect, decorator and landscape architect and set them to work. Versailles took 50 years to build. Hills were removed, marshes drained, water diverted from the Seine to feed the spectacular fountains. In 1685, three years after the court moved in, 36,000 workmen were still at the job. The court at Versailles included more than 1,000 nobles and their 4,000 servants, living in the palace with the king—plus soldiers, more servants, and hangers-on who filled the out-buildings and the town—some 20,000 people in all. A rigid etiquette was developed to keep this mob in hand, and to keep them safely dependent on royal favor. The court remained at Versailles during the reigns of Louis XV and Louis XVI. To escape its suffocating atmosphere Louis XV installed the intimate and lovely royal apartments and built the Grand Trianon. Louis XVI sought refuge in the Petit Trianon, and his queen Marie Antoinette fled daily to her pastoral village nearby where she and her friends played at being shepherdesses. After the execution of Louis XVI, the palace was deserted and began to crumble away. Demolition was discussed, but, instead, Versailles was turned into a museum, and restorations undertaken, the last after World War II. The parks and gardens are among Parisians' favorite Sunday promenades, especially in summer when twice a month— at fantastic expense—the great fountains play.

Chartres. The Cathedral of Chartres rises like a vision from the wheatfields of the Beauce. Approaching on the Ablis road, you

Skiers prepare for down-hill run, Val D'Isere, France.

will see its spire rising from the sea of wheat, an astonishing and moving introduction to this centuries-old "Acropolis of France." Considered by many experts to be the most beautiful cathedral in the world, Chartres is a masterpiece of medieval ecclesiastical architecture. The site has been a holy place since the days of the druids. A Roman temple was built here, and then, on its foundations, a Christian church rose in the 4th century, to be destroyed by fire in the 8th. Time and again, successive churches were destroyed by fire. Of the fifth church, built at the beginning of the 12th century, the right tower remains. The rest of the building dates from after the great fire of 1194. The crypts date from the 9th and 11th centuries, the superb Royal Portal from the 12th, the glorious stained-glass windows from the 12th and 13th, the left tower from the 16th. Both inside and outside the cathedral, Romanesque, Gothic and Renaissance styles blend into a remarkably serene and harmonious whole. You will want to look closely at the Gothic statues of the Royal Portal, to compare them with the Renaissance statues of the altar enclosure, and to examine the stained-glass windows, considered the most beautiful in the world. In the museum behind the church are tapestries, enamels, embroideries, armor—well worth seeing, as are the surrounding streets of old Chartres, particularly Rue de Bourg, Rue des Ecuyers, and Rue St. Pierre.

Maintenon. The interior of the chateau is still furnished as it was in the time of its most famous occupant, Mme de Maintenon, who was first the governess of the children of Louis XIV, later became his morganatic wife. The chateau was a gift to her from the king. She later gave it to her niece whose descendants live here still.

Rambouillet. The 14th-century chateau of Rambouillet has witnessed a grand parade of the rulers of France, who came here sometimes as owners, sometimes as guests. Francis I died at Rambouillet in 1547. The chateau was then the home of the captain of his body guard; feeling unwell, the king had stopped here on his return from a hunting trip. Louis XIV commandeered the chateau for one of his sons. Later, Louis XV was a frequent guest. Fond of the hunting offered nearby, Louis XVI bought

Pont-du-Gard stands as a monument to Romans who built it about 1000 years ago, Provence, France.

Rambouillet, but his enthusiasm for it was not shared by his queen, Marie Antoinette. Napoleon lived at Rambouillet for a time with Marie-Louise, and spent one of his last nights here before setting out on the long journey that was to end on Ste. Helena. The chateau is today one of the residences of the President of the Republic. When he is absent, the interior is open to the public.

Sèvres. Sèvres and porcelain are synonymous as you will discover if you visit the Porcelain Factory Museum. Here you will see examples of ceramic art and be able to buy contemporary pieces.

NORTHWEST OF PARIS

Malmaison. In the chateau of Malmaison, Josephine, wife of Napoleon, spent her happiest years with her husband, and her saddest years after their divorce. Malmaison, bought by her, was her personal property, and she spent lavishly—always reimbursed by her husband "for the last time"—to furnish the house and fill the garden with roses. All the furnishings are authentic. You may see the bed where she died, and a display of some of her 600 gowns. Less grandiose, certainly, than other Napoleonic shrines, Malmaison is by far the most evocative, the most moving, the most human.

St. Germain-en-Laye. In the old fortress, Francis I was married—but it did not conform to his ideas of royal splendor, so he had most of it demolished and rebuilt as his residence the chateau that stands today. St. Germain has also witnessed a royal parade—of both French and English sovereigns. Henry II and Louis XIV were born here; Louis XIII died here. Mary Stuart, Queen of Scots, lived here from the age of 6 to 16. The last year, she was Queen of France as well, but her young husband, Francis II, died within 12 months, and she returned to her own country to pursue her tragic destiny. After the French court had moved to Versailles, James II of England spent the final years of his exile here. Today the chateau houses an excellent museum devoted to prehistory and to Celtic and Gallo-Roman periods. From the

Lace-makers carry on their centuries-old craft, Pevy, France.

chateau's terrace there is a magnificent view across the Seine to Paris.

Maisons-Laffitte. The 17th-century chateau of Maisons was built by the famous architect Mansart, with an eye toward the royal visitors he knew it would receive. Among its guests were Louis XIV, Louis XV, Mme de Pompadour, Mme du Barry, Louis XVI, Marie Antoinette. It is the chateau's 19th-century owner, however, who gave it its present name—the banker Laffitte. Today all is in perfect condition—the tapestries, the paintings, the furniture.

Marly-le-Roi. Like London's Whitehall Palace, Marly is a favorite royal residence that has vanished. Louis XIV, a bit appalled by what he had created at Versailles, sought a country home to which he could escape from the etiquette and the crowd. Mansart designed for him a royal pavilion surrounded by 12 others, like signs of the zodiac surrounding the sun. The Sun King was delighted, and visited Marly with his chosen friends as often as he could. An invitation to join the king at Marly was an extreme honor. Wealth and titles were not enough; one had to be an agreeable guest by virtue of personality and conversation. The king himself made out the guest-list. Hunting, walking, gambling, concerts and balls were held at Marly, under far less rigorous etiquette than at Versailles, but in no greater comfort. Heating and sanitation remained a problem, despite the personal supervision of the king. Although Versailles was the official royal residence, Marly was the favorite royal residence of Louis XIV. Louis XV and Louis XVI visited it only sporadically. After the revolution, Marly was sold to a manufacturer who turned these pavilions into cotton mills, and eventually had them demolished. Only the park remains today, but if you are susceptible to French history, it is worth a visit.

Les Andelys. High above the Seine on the road to Rouen are the remains of Château Gaillard, the "impregnable fortress" of Richard the Lion-Hearted, King of England and Duke of Normandy. Begun in 1196 to prevent the French king Philippe-

Huge floats are part of the festivities at the Carnival in Nice, France.

Auguste from taking Rouen and finished the following year, the fortress remained unchallenged until Richard's death. In 1203-04 it was besieged by a terrible, silent ring of troops who attempted to starve it into submission. That failing, the keep was eventually penetrated through the latrine ducts. Besieged from within and without, the fortress finally fell. There are considerable ruins to climb about, and the views over the Seine valley are magnificent enough to convince you that you are Duke of Normandy and more than a match for any king of France.

NORTH OF PARIS

St-Denis. In the industrial suburb of today is the church where for centuries the kings of France were buried. The Basilica of St-Denis, built upon the sepulcher of the patron saint of Paris, has received their bodies since Dagobert was buried here in 638. Some of the present church dates from the 13th century. Francis I, Catherine de Medici, Henry II, the Louis and their queens were all buried here. You will still see the tombs bearing their images, but during the Revolution the royal remains were removed and flung into a common grave.

Chantilly. The superb 15th-century illuminated manuscript called "The Very Rich Hours of the Duc de Berri" is in the chateau museum, and is, itself, worth the trip. But Chantilly is also famous for its lace, its cream, its race track and stables, and a suicide. The suicide was that of the great chef Vatel. Maître-d'hôtel for the lord of the chateau during a visit of Louis XIV, Vatel had not slept for days in his eagerness to see that all was perfectly prepared. Instead, everything went wrong. Finally, when the fish failed to arrive, he could bear his shame no longer, and went to his room where he drove his sword through his body. In the chateau museum are also splendid collections of paintings, tapestries, miniatures and jewels, all worth seeing, for you will never see them elsewhere. Chantilly was bequeathed to the Institut de France on condition that its treasures were never to be loaned.

Shepherds in Landes region traditionally wear stilts to keep from sinking into soft earth.

Senlis. This ancient, small and tranquil town surrounded by a beech forest is rich in history and monuments. Its Gothic cathedral, begun in 1153, is older than Notre-Dame of Paris. The Royal Palace, now in ruins, was a residence of the kings of France from Charlemagne to Henry IV, and it was here in 987, after the death of the last Carolingian king, that Hughes Capet was named his successor and the line of Capetian kings began. In addition to Roman ruins, including an arena, there is a hunting museum (Musée de la Vénerie), unique in Europe. The ancient streets are worth exploring.

Pierrefonds. The fairytale castle you see today is a 19th-century reconstruction, by the famous Viollet-le-Duc, but so systematically achieved that it presents an excellent idea of a feudal castle.

Compiègne. It was to Compiègne, and to Fontainebleau, surrounded by two of the most magnificent forests in France, that Senlis lost its royal residents. Though the site of Compiègne greatly pleased the kings of France, its 14th-century castle was hardly suitable as a royal palace in the 17th century, and drew from Louis XIV the comment that at Versailles he lived like a king, at Fontainebleau like a prince, at Compiègne like a peasant. He had the chateau enlarged, and his successor, Louis XV ordered a thorough reconstruction. It was at Compiègne that Joan of Arc was captured in 1430. Here in 1770 the future Louis XVI, not yet king, saw his bride-to-be Marie Antoinette for the first time, and here in 1810 her niece, Marie-Louise of Austria, married Napoleon. Compiègne was also the favorite residence of Napoleon III and the Empress Eugénie. The interior of the castle, with its tapestries and fine collection of Empire furnishings, is of particular interest. There is also a museum showing carriages, bicycles, and cars of all periods. In the town is a beautiful 16th-century Hôtel de Ville built by Louis XII. In it are two interesting museums, one containing 85,000 lead, tin, and wooden soldiers. Near Compiègne is the Clairière de l'Armistice, where, in a railway coach run out on a special line, the Armistice of 1918 was signed, and, in 1940, the French surrender to Hitler.

Beautiful formal gardens are part of castle that inspired legend of "Sleeping Beauty," Château d'Usée, France.

Beauvais. The magnificent cathedral of Beauvais miraculously survived the bombing of June 1940 that destroyed much of the city. One of the most beautiful cathedrals anywhere, it is also one of the world's most ambitious architectural undertakings. In 1225 the religious leaders of Beauvais set out to build the largest and the tallest cathedral in the world. Stupendous technical problems and chronic lack of funds thwarted the project. It took 25 years to complete the soaring choir, another 40 to keep it from collapsing. The transept was finally completed in 1550, financed partly by the sale of indulgences. Then, instead of constructing the nave, the builders decided to top the transept with a steeple. Lacking the buttressing that would have been provided by the nave, it stood for only 4 years, crashing to the ground in 1573. With it crashed the dreams of Beauvais. The cathedral remains unfinished, without steeple, without nave. Even unfinished it is a spectacular sight, as are its tapestries and 13th and 14th century stained-glass windows. The famous needle point industry was destroyed during World War II. The tapestry workers have moved to the Gobelins Factory in Paris.

EAST OF PARIS

To the east of Paris lies the Valley of the Marne, a battlefield since the time of Julius Caesar, and scene of some of the great battles of World War I. It was to support the British in the first great battle of the Marne to which the French brought 6,000 troops from Paris in 600 taxis, each making the dangerous trip twice. The valley today is green and still, its many hilltops offering lovely views that belie its violent history.

Meaux. In this market center is a 13th-century cathedral which provides a maximum view of the valley from its tower. In the cathedral is the tomb of Bossuet, bishop and confessor to Louis XIV, as well as his tutor. In June of 1791, Louis XVI, Marie Antoinette and their children spent their last night of freedom at the bishopric here during their unsuccessful attempt to flee from the Revolution.

Château Maintenon, built by Louis XIV for one of his favorites, stands in the Loire Valley, France.

Château-Thierry. This is the birthplace of the famous writer of fables, La Fontaine, as well as the scene of some of the great battles in which American troops took part in World War I. Nearby at Belleau Wood is the American military cemetery, where 2,500 white crosses stretch row after row across the neat green lawns.

Returning to Paris, you may visit two small but interesting chateaux: Guermantes, whose name was borrowed by Marcel Proust in his famous novel *A La Recherche du Temps Perdu;* and Champs, whose most famous tenant was Mme de Pompadour, and which is now a summer residence of the French President.

SOUTHEAST OF PARIS

Fontainebleau. The famous and beautiful forest of Fontainebleau has been immortalized by the painters Corot, Millet, and Rousseau, who settled in the village of Barbizon nearby, thus immortalizing the name of the village as well. From Roman times to the present, the forest has been a wonderful place to hunt. Modern highway signs continue to mark stag and boar crossings, and during the winter you may meet hunts with hounds and horns. Like many another chateau, the royal palace of Fontainebleau owes its origin to the royal passion for hunting. A royal hunting lodge was established here in the 12th century, and from it grew the palace the stands today. In the 16th century, Francis I transformed the medieval chateau into a Renaissance palace, bringing specialists from Italy to direct the work of an army of decorators and painters. Among the masterpieces which the king imported from Italy to grace the palace was the *Mona Lisa.* Henry II continued his father's work on the palace, decorating it conspicuously with his initials interlaced with a D for Diane de Poitiers, his mistress. Henry IV, Louis XIV, and Louis XVI added their own remodelings and enlargements, as did Napoleon. Since you may still see the work completed by each successive generation of kings, Fontainebleau is in a sense a far more significant monument than Versailles. The great gallery and ballroom of Francis I, the beautiful apartments of Marie An-

Castle appears eerily lit during "sound and light" spectacle, Langeais Château, Loire Valley, France.

toinette, the private apartments of Napoleon and Josephine are only a few of the highlights. You will also want to see the famous Court of Adieux, where Napoleon bade farewell to his Guard before his departure for Elba.

Provins. During the Middle Ages, Provins was, after Paris and Rouen, the most important city in France, and its fairs were famous throughout Europe. The city was also famous for the culture of red roses, introduced in France by returning Crusaders. Provins holds a curious place in English history. The red rose of Provins became a part of the coat of arms of the English House of Lancaster in the 13th century, when a Count of Lancaster became by marriage also a Count of Provins. The flower was the symbol of Lancaster 150 years later, in the famous Wars of Roses. Provins today is an extremely picturesque and interesting town, with many reminders of its feudal past, including fine ramparts, a church, and a keep, all dating from the 12th century.

Vaux-le-Vicomte. This magnificent chateau is one of the great monuments of 17th-century architecture, as well as the scene of one of history's most dazzling and disastrous parties. The chateau and its beautiful park were designed by the foremost artists of the day for Fouquet, Finance Minister of France, who was none too scrupulous about the distinction between public and personal funds. Desiring a chateau that would reflect his success, Fouquet gave his artists absolutely free rein. When the chateau was completed, he inaugurated it with a reception in honor of his young king, Louis XIV. There were 80 tables, 30 buffets, 6,400 pieces of silver service and, on the king's table, a service of solid gold. After the dinner, created by the ubiquitous Vatel, the guests repaired to the enormous gardens where they were entertained by ballets, concerts, a new play by Molière, and fireworks, all set amid the 1,200 sparkling fountains and cascades. It was a party of great brilliance—and Louis XIV, furious at being outshone, banished Fouquet, confiscated his wealth, commandeered his artists, and set out in a rage to build Versailles. The chateau is open March through October. Walking through the gardens you will find it easy to visualize the grandeur of its past history. If you

Pines frame facade of Château de Blois, Loire Valley, France.

are interested in Versailles, you must not miss Vaux-le-Vicomte,
which started it all.

THE PROVINCES

"But Paris is not France!" your traveling friends will insist. More
accurately, it is not all of France, by any means, any more than
New York or San Francisco is all of the United States. To savor
France, you should see its countryside, its towns and villages, its
castles, coasts, resorts, a festival, a pilgrimage.

You may be amazed by the diversity of France, and of the
French. In the north, in Normandy, the people are often blond,
serious-minded, industrious, while their compatriots to the south
are Mediterranean in appearance and temperament, often dark-
haired, dark-eyed, volatile, more carefree in their attitude toward
life. But generalizations are dangerous—particularly about the
French. You must see for yourself.

Where you will go in France depends, of course, on what you
want to see, what appeals to your tastes and interests. For
colorful customs, rugged Atlantic coastal scenery, you should
visit Brittany. For hedgerows, history, rich and delicious dining,
try Normandy. For placid countryside, magnificent chateaux, see
the Valley of the Loire. But there is so much—so much to see and
do everywhere! The Alps, the Pyrenees, the Riviera, the vineyards of Bordeaux, Champagne and Burgundy, Roman France
along the Rhône. In the Camargue, you will even find French
cowboys.

To help you decide what you would like to see, here are brief
descriptions of the various provinces and regions of France. The
countryside invites your exploration. You will always find
something interesting to look at, something enjoyable to do, a
pleasant place to stay, a good place to eat.

The visual beauty of France is astonishing, for where its
natural beauty has been touched by man, it has not been defaced,
but incorporated, to produce a blend of nature, art and artifice
that can be breath-taking.

It is virtually impossible to take a wrong road in France—or to
stick to a fixed itinerary. There is always something to discover,
an inviting detour, a festival in the next town, a castle on the next
hill.

Aerial view of the Chambord, famed for its use as a hunting lodge
Kings and nobles, Loire Valley, France.

BRITTANY

Geography and history have combined to make Brittany unique among the provinces. Like the prow of France, it cuts into the sea —the English Channel to the north, the Atlantic to the west and south. Its people are descendents of the Celts, who by inclination and their comparative isolation from the rest of France have retained the ancient Breton language, picturesque customs and colorful traditions that give Brittany its special charm.

The variety of Brittany's 750-mile coastline typifies the variety found in the entire region. Spectacular cliffs pounded by surf alternate with safe and sandy beaches, placid coves, with treacherous tidal bays. Inland, the landscape is sometimes wild, barren and mist-shrouded, sometimes almost subtropical, dotted with palms and mimosa.

If there seems to be a touch of Cornwall in the crags, moors and coves of Brittany and in the Bretons themselves, there is good reason. The settlers of Brittany came from Cornwall more than 1500 years ago as refugees from the Danish and Saxon invasions, bringing with them their legends, as well as their language and their way of life. Memories of Tristan and Isolde hover in the air of Brittany as in that of Cornwall; the legendary home of King Arthur's magician Merlin is the Breton wood of Paimpont. And Brittany too has its Land's End, called Finistère.

Mist, mystery, and mysticism are all to be found in Brittany. But nowhere do they blend more strangely than at Carnac, where thousands of prehistoric megaliths stretch across the moors— enormous stones laid out in rows and patterns, no one knows by whom, or when, or how, or why.

A landscape fertile for the imagination, the ever-present danger of the sea, and their Celtic origin do much to explain the Bretons' mystical sense and fervent religious feeling. Evidences of their belief are everywhere—in the innumerable parish churches, the calvaries, the blessing of the fishing fleets, and especially in the famous local pilgrimages called *pardons*, which celebrate various saints' days. For these, and for the frequent folk festivals, many Breton women still wear their traditional costume with its lacy white or colored headdress.

Chamonix cable car carries tourists and vacationers through the French Alps, France.

Brittany has given France one of its most famous authors, Chateaubriand, and its best sailors, including the famous Jacques Cartier, discoverer of the St. Lawrence.

Many of its coastal towns are ancient pirate strongholds.

All the pleasures of the sea are offered in Brittany. The resorts along its sandy beaches range from the large and fashionable such as La Baule and Dinard to countless modest "family beaches" and picturesque fishing ports. Tuna, salmon and trout fishing are excellent.

Many of the regional specialties, too, are from the sea. Particularly delicious are the oysters, crab, sole, a tiny succulent shrimp called *crevette,* and rock lobster, frequently creamed in a style called either *à l'armoricaine, or à l'américaine.* Other specialties include mutton with beans, strawberries, artichokes, macaroons, and Breton pastry, especially *crêpe dentelle.* The local dry, white Muscadet wine goes well with the seafood; another specialty is cider.

The most interesting part of Brittany lies west of Saint-Brieuc and Vannes. In this far end of the peninsula customs and traditions have been most authentically retained. Here you will see the customs, hear the Breton language, and witness interesting *pardons,* which are unique religious ceremonies.

La Baule is one of the great seaside resorts of France. Here you'll find a six-mile stretch of sand beach, with all the attendant amenities—luxury hotels, an active social life, casino, villas, gardens. At either end of La Baule are the family resorts of Pornichet and Le Pouliguen, which offer a bit less chic at less expense.

Concarneau is a 14th-century walled town enclosed by towers and ramparts. Tuna and sardine boats contribute to the animation of its active harbor.

Dinan is an old and charming town, with a 14th-century fortified castle, and a 15th-century church, Saint-Sauveur. From the town's ramparts and parks there is a lovely view over the Rance Valley. Old houses and old streets add to the attraction of this Breton town.

Cathedral at Amiens

Dinard has its own delights, but not to be confused with those of Dinan. A chic and social resort with sandy beach, Dinard offers golf, pools, casinos, subtropical vegetation, a fine view of St. Malo.

Saint-Malo, an ancient pirate stronghold, is another centuries-old walled city. During World War II, it lost its cathedral and many of the pirate houses along the walls—burned during the German stand here against General Patton in August 1944, as were three-fourths of its buildings. But much has been restored in the old style, and much of interest is still intact: the enormous ramparts with their sweeping views, the medieval chateau. You may also see St. Malo's historical figures in the Quic-en-Groigne wax-works, enjoy the sandy beaches, visit the Ile du Grand-Beq with its tomb of Chateaubriand and majestic vistas along the coast. St. Malo is a good starting point for interesting excursions, and the site of a great *pardon* in February.

Perros-Guirec is a well-known Channel resort with a Breton flavor. Here there is an important *pardon* on August 15. In addition to the casino and fine beaches, there is also an active port.

Brest, almost totally destroyed during the Second World War, is being rebuilt as a light and spacious city, though rather removed from traditional Breton style. From the 13th-century castle of this old and important port there are fine views over the harbor.

Fougères has a fine 11th- and 15th-century chateau that is one of the best examples of medieval military architecture in all of Europe.

Quimper is famous for the pottery that bears its name, as the center of a region rich in natural beauty and archeological interest, and as a Breton city of charm in its own right. The capital of ancient Cornouaille, it contains unusual examples of 16th-century city planning, a 13th-century cathedral, and an

The sweeping shore line of Nice as seen from a field of daisies

excellent art museum particularly rich in examples of the Dutch school. There is also a museum of Breton history, archeology, and folklore in the former Episcopal Palace. Quimper is a starting point for interesting excursions—to Pleyben, famous for its calvary; to Pont-Aven, where Paul Gauguin did much of his early painting, and where there is the outstanding festival of the Golden Gorse in August; and to Pointe du Raz, the most spectacular of the cliff-ends of Brittany, where savage waves pound the jagged rocks and the panoramic views of the Breton coast are magnificent. One of Brittany's major folk festivals is held in Quimper during July, the Festival of the Queens of Cornwall.

Vannes is one of the oldest towns of Brittany, with ancient fortifications, old streets with old houses that retain the Breton atmosphere, a 13th- to 18th-century cathedral, gardens, and a museum of local prehistory. Vannes is also a starting point for some of the most interesting excursions in Brittany. At nearby Josselin is Brittany's finest castle, ancestral home of the de Rohan family, with its towers mirrored in the waters of the Oust River. At Ste. Anne-d'Auray, on July 26th, there is an important *pardon*. At Carnac stand more than 3,000 megaliths, carefully laid across a fifteen-mile area by a prehistoric people. Several of the gigantic stones weigh hundreds of tons; modern man has no idea how these enormous monuments were transported, raised, and erected. There is also an interesting and typically Breton church, a prehistoric museum, and, at Carnac Plage, a pleasant beach. The Quiberon peninsula is extremely scenic, with fishing ports and beaches along its wild coast.

Vitré is one of the towns in France that has best kept its medieval appearance, with old houses supported on pillars, one of the finest of the remaining 11th-century castles, and tower-studded ramparts.

Nantes, Brittany's major city, was severely damaged in the Second World War. Its imposing 15th-century castle, the old residence of the Dukes of Brittany, now houses an extremely

138

The French Riviera view of Tourette-sur-Loup

interesting folklore museum. The Fine Arts Museum contains a rich and beautiful collection of paintings. From Nantes, boat trips may be taken along the Loire, the Erdre and the Sevre.

Hotels and Restaurants
Note: Many hotels and restaurants along the coast are open during the summer months only.

La Baule: Hotel Hermitage, deluxe; Castel Marie-Louise, the Royal, both first class; Toque Blanche, Christina, comfortable; Armoric, moderate; Toque Blanche Hotel has good restaurant; L'Espadon, Chez Henri for seafood specialties.

Brest: Hotel Voyageurs (good restaurant); Regina and Grappe de Raisin, good kitchens.

Dinan: Poste Hotel, good restaurant (also six rooms); 18 miles away at Hede is Hostellerie du Vieux Moulin.

Dinard: Grande Hotel, first class; Printania has pretty setting; Try Grand Hotel restaurant and Roche Corneille at Coquille for food.

Perros-Guirec: There are three first class hotels with nice views and good food—The Grand Hotels de Trestraou, the Primtania and the Morgane; the Sphinx, good food and view; Rochers good, small, reservations needed.

Pont-Aren: Moulin Rosmadec is reconstructed mill in rustic setting beside a pretty stream with very superior cuisine.

Quimper: Eppe and Pascal et Terminus good hotels, restaurants; Tour d'Auvergne also good.

Rennes: Central, President and Astrid Hotels—no restaurants; Du Gueselin Hotel—restaurant; restaurants Ti-Koz, Corsaire.

Carnac is at the centre of an immense area of magaliths which along 15 miles of the coast are scattered over field and moorland

Saint-Malo: Central Hotel, first class; Chez Chuche, Duchesse Anne, good food; the Panoramic in the Casino, good.

Nantes: Hotel Duchesse Anne and Central Hotels have good restaurants. Many interesting restaurants to explore: La Rotisserie, Coq Hardi, Chez Biret; the Park and Mon Reve, excellent.

NORMANDY

The great province of Normandy is one of the richest in France, and one of the most rewarding for the foreign visitor. From the famous ports of Dieppe, Le Havre, and Cherbourg, its lush orchards, fields, and pastures spread toward Paris. The superb Bayeux tapestries are here, as are Mont-Saint-Michel, perhaps the most spectacular sight in all of France, and Deauville, one of the country's most lavish resorts. Amid these treasures and pleasures are names that ring in French, English, and American history—Rouen, Harfleur, Omaha, and Utah beaches.

Normandy is the natural invasion route from the Channel to Paris. For more than a thousand years, its coast and countryside have been battlegrounds, as war followed war for the possession of the prize of Normandy. First settled by the Viking Northmen who gave it its name, Normandy has been disputed territory since its seventh and most famous Duke William defeated the Saxon king Harold at the Battle of Hastings in 1066, winning for himself both the throne of England and the name of Conqueror. Defending his title of Duke of Normandy, Richard the Lion-Hearted withstood the French king here. After two more centuries of alternate battle and truce, England's Henry V reconquered Normandy emphatically at the Battle of Agincourt. But peace was not to last, and the claims to Normandy were not settled definitively until the 19th century. With the Allied landings in 1944, Normandy became a battlefield again.

Many of Normandy's shattered cities have been restored or rebuilt, but much remains as it has been for centuries—hedgerows and half-timbered houses, villas and farms in the style that is distinctively "Norman," Romanesque churches and abbeys of the Benedictine monks. Above all, Normandy's prosperity remains, in fact as well as appearance. Agriculture, fishing,

Skiers skim down Mt. Blanc into the valley of Chamonix

shipping thrive, and the bright landscape is serene in this historic and scenic province.

You will dine prodigiously in Normandy, for it is a gastronome's paradise. From its pastures, fields, and orchards come some of France's great specialties—the cheeses *Pont l'Evêque*, *Livarot*, and *Camembert*, the apple brandy *Calvados*, Benedictine liqueur. Normandy is France's dairy land, with excellent butter and delicious heavy cream that is the base of many sauces, particularly the *sauce normande*. Beef, seafood, poultry are also excellent. Among the best-known regional dishes are *tripe à la mode de Caen*, *sole normande*, *omelette Mère-Poulard* (at Mont-Saint-Michel), *poulet Vallée d'Auge* (chicken with tiny onions), *canard à la Rouennaise* (pressed duck), *médaillon à la normande* (creamed veal). The regional drink is a delicious, sparkling cider.

Of all the famous French provinces, Normandy is the most quickly and easily accessible from Paris. It is a great holiday favorite of both foreigners and the French, including the Normans.

Alençon is famous for the lace to which it has given its name. A fine collection is displayed at the museum in Place Foch. A school of lace, 13 Rue du Pont Neuf, may also be visited. The Late Gothic church of Notre-Dame has a fine porch and interesting 16th-century stained-glass windows. At 40 Rue St. Blaise is the birthplace of St. Theresa of Lisieux. Alençon is in the midst of a renowned horse-breeding region. Nearby, at Haras du Pin, is one of the world's famous stud farms, built in 1714 from designs by Mansart, and owned by the state. You may visit the stables where some 400 of the finest horses in France are kept. Also near Alençon is the vast 16th-century chateau of Carrouges, one of the most famous of the Norman chateaux, an imposing mass of buildings surrounded by a rectangular moat.

Bayeux spans 900 years of the history of war; it should not be missed. In its Tapestry Museum is the superb 11th-century embroidery variously known as the "Bayeux Tapestry" and "Queen Matilda's Tapestry" that depicts, in 58 scenes, the

Devolry

events leading to the conquest of England, the invasion, and the battle of Hastings. Commissioned shortly after 1066, either by William the Conqueror's queen Matilda or by his half-brother the Bishop of Bayeux, it is 231 feet long by 19 inches wide. The extraordinary vividness of the episodes and the exactitude with which men, horses, ships, and weapons are portrayed make it fascinating to both layman and historian. Only a few miles from the town are the sites of the Allied invasion of 1944. At Arromanches, remains of the incredible artificial harbor "Mulberry" are to be seen, and there are films and a diorama of the landings in the large, modern museum. Farther west are Omaha Beach and Utah Beach, where the great landings were made. Omaha Beach and Pointe du Hoc, nearby, provide the most vivid and moving reminders of D-Day and the days that followed. The town of Bayeux was the first in France to be liberated, miraculously undamaged. The huge cathedral is a fine example of Norman art, and the winding ancient streets of Rue Bourbesneur, Rue des Cuisiniers, Rue des Chanoines near the cathedral are charming.

Caen, despite heavy wartime damage, still contains some fine ancient buildings, and still merits its name of "city of spires." Caen was the seat of William the Conqueror. The sober and splendid monastery of Abbaye aux Hommes was built by him in 1066, as part of the price he paid for the lifting of an excommunication that followed his marriage to his cousin, Matilda. She, in turn, founded the Abbaye aux Dames, at the other end of the town, of which the crypt and pillars remain. The churches of Saint Pierre and Saint Nicolas are fine examples of Norman craftsmanship. Like the abbeys, they withstood the bombardments of 1944, while buildings around them fell.

Cherbourg was the first deep-water port to become available to the Allies in 1944, and became the terminal of PLUTO, the pipeline under the ocean, through which fuel was pumped from England. The rebuilt harbor is once again one of the leading ports-of-call of France. Cherbourg is most interesting as an excursion center for the wild and beautiful Cotentin Peninsula, tipped by the Nez de Jobourg, where the 500-foot sea cliffs are the highest in Europe.

Fish market at Nice

The view encompasses the Channel islands of Jersey and Guernsey; the sea seems tranquil, but it is one of the most dangerous stretches of water along the Normandy coast. Here, as elsewhere in Normandy and Brittany, low water reveals tempting stretches of beach that invite exploration—but tides and weather are hazardous and unpredictable. Never venture down the cliffs and along the shore without a reliable local guide.

Coutances is noted for its magnificent 13th-century cathedral that can be seen from 30 miles around. An interesting perspective effect makes the public gardens appear much larger than they are, and from their terraces there is a fine view over the valley.

Deauville-Trouville are two of France's most fashionable resorts, the former in the present tense, the latter in the past. Artists, writers, and eventually the aristocracy made Trouville the leading resort of the mid-19th century. Soon after, pleasure seekers, wishing something more exclusive, began to build their villas across the river Touques, and so launched Deauville, which remains one of the most fashionable resorts in France. Trouville, old-fashioned, inexpensive, a bit motley, contrasts strongly with its haughty sister, frequented by millionaires, princes, diplomats, and starlets. Deauville offers casinos, palatial hotels, regattas, horse-racing, sports car rallies, golf, luxurious shops, swimming, and a new marina.

Dieppe is both an active port and a seaside resort. Its 16th-century resident, the banker and shipbuilder Jean Ango, financed the exploratory voyages of Verrazano to the mid-Atlantic regions of North America. There is a 15th-century castle with fine woodwork, and a museum containing ivory ornaments and early navigational instruments.

Falaise is the birthplace of William the Conqueror. In the castle, the conquest of England was planned. There is a fine 12th-century keep, and a 13th-century tower, illuminated in Sound and Light performances during the summer. Between Falaise and

The Palace of the Popes in Avignon

Vire lies the area known as Norman Switzerland, a delightfully scenic region of valleys, forests, and gorges, ideal for picnicking, hiking, fishing. Clécy is the tourist center of the area.

Fécamp is an important fishing port with an imposing abbey, where, according to legend, drops of Christ's blood are treasured. Benedictine liqueur is distilled here (you can visit the plant), and there is a museum of Benedictine history.

Le Havre, one of the major ports of France, was nearly flattened during World War II. A new city has risen from the ashes of the old, a marvel of town planning with a fine modern port that may be visited by free boat tour. Nearby are two of the most famous and colorful ports of France of long-ago. Honfleur, just across the Seine, is one of the most picturesque towns in all of Normandy, with ancient streets and houses, including the old dock area and the Lieutenance, once the residence of the local governor. The wooden church of Sainte Catherine was built by ships' carpenters, who were unwilling to wait for laggard stone masons. Harfleur, on the Le Havre bank, was immortalized by Shakespeare as the site of Henry V's battle speech that begins, "Once more unto the breach, dear friends, once more . . ."

Jumièges abbey, founded in the 7th century, became one of the most important in the west. Destroyed and rebuilt during the following centuries, vandalized during the Revolution, it is today an imposing and spectacular ruin, one of the most beautiful in Normandy.

Lisieux, an industrial town, the object of world-wide pilgrimage, contains the house where Saint Theresa spent her childhood, the convent which she entered in 1888 and where she died in 1897, and the chapel that houses her remains. Also here are Saint Theresa's family home, *Les Buissonets*, and the 12th- and 13th-century cathedral of Saint-Pierre.

Mont-Saint-Michel is an island of rock, almost completely covered by an abbey church, cloisters, courtyards, stairways,

Le Puy
The chapel of St.-Michel-d'Aiguihle is precariously perched on a 260 ft. volcanic needle

ramparts. The ensemble is one of the most spectacular sights in France and in the world. On this spot in the 8th century, the Archangel Michel appeared to advise the building of a sanctuary. From the original chapel there grew, over the next ten centuries, a fantastic complex of buildings that achieve a serene fairy-tale beauty. The buildings are terraced one above the other, with the towers of the abbey church, perched on the point of the rocky pinnacle, soaring above all into the clouds. This was the only fortress that held for the French king when the victorious English armies swept over Normandy after the victory at Agincourt. Discontinued as a monastery after the Revolution, Mont-Saint-Michel did duty as a prison during the Napoleonic era. Today it is classified as an historical monument and is the object of innumerable pilgrimages. After you climb the single street, you will want to see the abbey church, the ''lace stairs,'' the ''Wonder,'' and especially its lovely cloister, the gardens, and the ramparts. Mont-Saint-Michel is reached by a causeway. At low tide, the sea withdraws as much as ten miles, leaving the Mont surrounded by a smooth, inviting beach that stretches as far as the eye can see. To venture on it, however, is to risk your life. Quicksands abound, fog may appear on the clearest day, and when the irregular tide comes rushing in, it advances at a phenomenal rate of more than 200 feet a minute. The finest views of the Mont are to be had from Avranches, on the mainland eight miles to the northwest, particularly from the Botanical Garden (*Jardin des Plantes*) and from the esplanade.

Rouen, capital of Normandy, contains one of the greatest cathedrals in France, and is the city where, on May 30, 1431, Joan of Arc was burned at the stake. On the Place du Vieux-Marché, you may see the spot where she died, marked by a plaque. Severely damaged during the Second World War, the 13th-century cathedral has been painstakingly reconstructed. You will also want to see the fine Renaissance clock tower (*La Grosse Horloge*), and the medieval Palais de Justice. Rouen's Musée des Beaux-Arts is one of France's finest museums, with a *splendid* collection of paintings and ceramics. At Musée le Secq des Tournelles are exhibits of ironwork, including grills, gates, keys,

The first sight of Carcassone and its walls is one of the great experiences that the world offers to tourists

stair rails. There are also museums devoted to Joan of Arc, and to Flaubert and Corneille, two of France's most famous writers who were natives of Rouen. Like Paris, Rouen spans the Seine. From Bonsecours, high on the corniche road above the river, there are breath-taking views of Rouen and Normandy.

Hotels and Restaurants
Note: Many of the beach resort hotels and restaurants are open from May through September only.

Alençon: Grand Cerf, first class; Gare, moderately priced; Petit Vatel, excellent restaurant.

Bayeux: Hotel Lion d'Or, good hotel, good restaurant.

Caen: Hotel Malherbe with its good restaurant; Le Rabelais; Hotel Moderne and Hotel France.

Cherbourg: Sofitel at Gare Maritime, with view of port; Moderne, good and moderately priced; Toque Blanche and Café du Theatre, good seafood restaurants.

Deauville: Famed Normandy Hotel is elegant, faces the sea and is open year round; Royal on the beach is deluxe; the Golf delightfully situated on the golf course; Arcades, Castel Normand and Royal, very good; The Grill Room in the Casino and Chez Augusto for food.

Dieppe: Hotels La Presidence, Univers, Windsor; the Horizon restaurant at the Casino good and Marmite Dieppoise.

Etretat: Golf Hotel, Dormy House, near golf course with nice view of beach; Angleterre Hotel has good restaurant.

Le Harve: Normandie Hotel; Le Monaco, small hotel, good food.

Honfleur: Chateau de la Roche Vasouy, good restaurant; Ferme Saint Simeon hotel and restaurant.

Colmar
All the charm of the late Middle-Ages and the early Renaissance are spread out like a feast before the visitor's eyes

Lisieux: Hotel and restaurant Esperana, first class; Grand Hotel Normandie, moderate; The Parc and LaTruite Normande, good food.

Mont-Saint-Michel: Mère Poulard, small, moderately priced, good dining room; Du Guesclin also small hotel same price range; try famous amelittes in Mère Poulard, Du Guesclin or Vieille Auberge.

Rouen: Hotels Angleterre, Poste are first class, good food; Astrid, moderate, no restaurant. Outstanding restaurants: Le Relais Fleuri, La Couronne, Michel and La Maree.

CHATEAU COUNTRY—THE LOIRE VALLEY

Southwest of Paris, the banks of the River Loire and its tributaries are lined with the most spectacular series of castles in all of France. From Gien to Angers, this is the unforgettable "chateau country," rich in art and history, and blessed with such soft and verdant beauty that it is often called the Garden of France.

Feudal fortresses rose here in the Middle Ages, and classical mansions in the 17th and 18th centuries, but it was during the 15th and particularly the 16th centuries that the most significant of the chateaux were built or came into their great days of splendor as residences of the kings of France.

From the reign of Charles VII (the timid Dauphin whose throne was secured by Joan of Arc) through the reign of Henry III, the Loire Valley was for 150 years the favorite royal abode.

Of the feudal fortresses, Angers, Cinon, Langeais, Loches, and Sully are the most famous.

Blois, Chambord, Amboise, Azay-le-Rideau, Chaumont, and Chenonceaux are the principal Renaissance chateaux—and the ones most people come to see. The first two were built as royal residences. The last four, built by nobles or great financiers of the era, were soon acquired by the Crown.

Cheverny and Valençay are the best examples of the later classical mansions.

Roman ruins rest quietly in the once bustling crossroads of Orange, France

Charles VII favored the fortress of Chinon, but his successors preferred the more luxurious settings of Amboise and Blois. Not satisfied with either of these, Francis I made extensive additions to both, and created for himself the immense chateau of Chambord. A man who liked to feel at home everywhere, Francis I also confiscated Azay-le-Rideau and Chenonceaux. The latter acquired its greatest fame, however, when his successor, Henri II, gave it to his celebrated mistress Diane de Poitiers. In her turn, Henri's widow, Catherine de Medici, acquired the far more austere Chaumont and in revenge exiled Diane de Poitiers there.

The history of the region comes brilliantly to life during the illuminations and *Son et Lumière* spectacles at many of the chateaux during the summer months.

Also in the area are the towns of Orléans, associated with Joan of Arc; Le Mans, scene of the famous Grand Prix road race in mid-June; Saumur, with its cavalry school; and Tours, principal excursion center for the district.

In 1940 and 1944, World War II swept through the Loire Valley, severely damaging many of the towns and villages. Though often threatened, the great chateaux were spared, frequently through dramatic effort and sacrifice. Blois, for example, was endangered by a fire that destroyed much of the town in 1940. To save the chateau from the flames, surrounding houses were blown up with dynamite.

Gastronomic specialties of the Loire include salmon, *aloses farcies* (stuffed shad), *truite au vouvray* (trout in wine), *pâté de Paques* (made of veal and pork), pike, sausage, and game—for this is fine hunting country. Most of the local wines are white— *Pouilly-sur-Loire, Reully, Muscadet, Vouvray, Saumur.* Good red wines are *Chinon* and *Bourgueil.* At Tours and Bourgueil, wine cellars may be visited.

The treasures of the Loire are best toured leisurely, over a period of a week or so, lest you suffer from a surfeit of chateaux. If time is limited, however, you can get a good general picture of the region by visiting Chinon, Amboise, Blois, Chambord, Chenonceaux, and Cheverny. Your enjoyment will be increased

Tilting windmills still can be seen in the countryside around Les Baux, the centuries-old hilltop village in Provence

immeasurably if you carry with you the excellent Michelin *Green Guide to the Chateaux of the Loire,* available in an English edition.

Amboise is one of the two great Renaissance chateaux most favored by the kings of France as a royal residence. Charles VIII was born here and died here. During his lifetime, enchanted by the palaces he had seen in Italy, he began to embellish the Gothic castle with Renaissance additions and décor. His work was continued by Louis XII and completed by Francis I, who spent his childhood and the early years of his reign at Amboise. This was the most brilliant period in its history—a time of tournaments, balls, and festivals. To add finishing touches to Amboise, Francis I brought Leonardo da Vinci from Italy. At the Clos-Luce, in the town, is the house where Leonardo lived during the last years of his life, and where he died. Francis I often visited him here, coming from the chateau by a recently-discovered underground passage. Amboise is now the property of the Count of Paris, claimant to the French throne.

Angers is the former capital of Anjou, seat of the Counts of Anjou from whom the Plantagenet line of kings of England were descended. Today, an important wine and market center with a population of about 135,000, Angers contains a fine feudal castle and a beautiful 12th- and 13th-century cathedral. Among the unique collection of tapestries displayed in the castle is the remarkable 14th-century "Apocalypse Tapestry," more than 350 feet long, and in itself worth the journey to Angers.

Azay-le-Rideau is one of the most graceful of the Renaissance chateaux. Built early in the 16th century by the treasurer to Francis I, its splendor contributed substantially to the former's downfall. In a series of episodes that foreshadowed the similar fate of the equally imprudent Fouquet, the King confiscated Azay, and sent his treasurer into exile. Unless you happened to be a king, building a palace fit for a king was not a good idea.

Blois is the second great Renaissance chateau that served as royal residence for a series of kings. Some of the building dates from the 13th and 15th centuries, but the finest part is the work of Francis I, who added the monumental open-framework staircase and the celebrated Italianate façade. Here, as elsewhere, Francis I brought the Renaissance to France. Seat of the Court continuously under Henri II and his three sons, Blois is extremely rich in history. One of France's more famous plots and counterplots culminated here in the assassination of the Duc de Guise on order of Henri III.

Chambord, created by Francis I as his personal palace, is by far the largest of the Loire chateaux, containing 440 rooms. Choosing a spot deep in the forest, the King saw to it that work on Chambord continued even when he lacked funds to ransom his sons from Spain. At one point he wished to divert the Loire to the foot of the chateau, but was persuaded to content himself with diverting a smaller river instead. Marvels of the chateau are a staircase of double spirals which never meet, and a magnificent roof terrace from which courtiers and their ladies could watch tournaments, and the departure and return of the hunt.

Chaumont is smaller, picturesque, but a bit grim and stern, with a touch of the fortress about its turrets and towers, as befits a place of exile. Diane de Poitiers lived here much against her will, and later Madame de Staël, exiled from Paris by Napoleon, spent some time here.

Chenonceaux, built over the River Cher, is perhaps the most beautiful of all the Loire chateaux, for its site is as romantic as its history. Erected by a financier in the era of Francis I, Chenonceaux, like Azay, fell quickly into royal hands. In 1547, Henri II presented it to his mistress, Diane de Poitiers, who added a garden and a bridge. Twelve years later, on the king's death, his widow Catherine de Medici took over the chateau and sent her rival to Chaumont. Catherine laid out another park, and built the two-story gallery on the bridge. Her young son, Francis II, and

his equally young wife, Mary, Queen of Scots, were among
Chenonceaux's later royal residents.

Cheverny is one of the lordly mansions of the Loire, built in the
17th century in the classical style, by the Count of Cheverny. It
remains in the family and, unlike Blois and Chambord, retains its
furnishings.

Chinon is a vast fortress from the Middle Ages, originally three
fortresses, in fact, separated by moats but protected by a
common rampart. Chinon holds memories of two kings of
England, Henry II and Richard the Lion-Hearted, and of the
latter's great adversary, Philippe-Auguste, King of France. Its
most famous day came in 1429, however, when Joan of Arc
sought out the Dauphin here, immediately recognized him though
he had exchanged robes with a courtier, and enlightened him of
her mission. Largely in ruin today, the chateau is still a beautiful
sight. In the town below it are interesting old streets, particularly
Rue Voltaire, which retains the atmosphere of the Middle Ages.

Fontevrault, midway between Chinon and Saumur, is often
overlooked on the circuit of chateaux, but should not be missed
by anyone with a taste for history. In the handsome 12th-century
Abbey are buried, by their own choice, some of the most famous
of the Plantagenet kings of England. Among them are King
Henry II and his wife Eleanor of Aquitaine, their son King
Richard the Lion-Hearted, and the wife of their other son, King
John. Simple and extremely moving effigies top the tombs. You
will also want to see the Abbey's fascinating Romanesque
kitchen, the only one in France. Though the Abbey is today a
prison—and you may be peered at by some of the inmates—the
tombs and kitchen may be visited with the warden as your guide.

Langeais is one of the finest of feudal military castles, begun in
1465. The interior is furnished in perfect period taste, presenting
a vivid picture of aristocratic life in the 15th century. In the
surrounding park is a 10th-century keep, the oldest in France.

Loches was established in the Middle Ages by the Counts of Anjou as a fortified political prison. Captured in a brilliant campaign by Richard the Lion-Hearted (who spent very little time back home in England), it was retaken by Philippe-Auguste ten years later. Agnès Sorel, beautiful favorite of Charles VII, lived here in the 15th century.

Le Mans, north of the Loire on the River Sarthe, is famous for its Grand Prix road race. It has a fine museum of paintings, and is an important town of some 120,000.

Orléans is an active business center, but best known as the city delivered from siege by Joan of Arc. She routed the English troops here in 1429. Almost a thousand years before, Orléans was besieged by Attila the Hun, but the city held, with Roman help, and the advance of the Huns was checked. There is an interesting fine arts museum, and an imposing cathedral.

Saumur is the home of the world-famous cavalry school established in 1763. Displays by its outstanding "Black Squadron" take place in July. The city also contains a majestic 14th-century castle housing a rich museum of decorative arts, and a unique museum devoted to the history of the horse.

Sully's great castle is the only one of those associated with Joan of Arc that still looks as it did in her day. From her victory at Orléans she came here to again persuade the Dauphin to be crowned. She returned to Sully in 1430 after her failure to take Paris. Her star descending, she remained a virtual prisoner in the great dark rooms for almost a month, and from here set out on her fateful journey which was to end at Compiègne.

Tours is the natural excursion center for the chateaux country, situated almost exactly between Angers and Orléans. Here is the tomb of St. Martin, former Roman legionnaire who became bishop of Tours in the 4th century and was largely responsible for converting the Gauls to Christianity. One of the decisive battles in world history took place here in 732, when Charles Martel defeated the Moors, checking forever the advance of Islam in the West. There is a very good fine arts museum, and interesting walks may be taken in the old part of town.

Ussé is the castle that inspired the story-teller Perrault to write "Sleeping Beauty." Even in this land of sumptuous chateaux its delightful fairy-tale appearance makes it well worth seeing.

Valançay is another of the great palaces built by financiers. Its mainly classical style is enhanced by its fine park where llamas, deer, peacocks, swans, and flamingos wander freely.

Villandry is a chateau most famous for its magnificent Renaissance gardens, unique in France. Its three terraces contain a water garden, an ornamental garden, and a vegetable garden, all meticulously arranged in geometric patterns. As a fitting background, there is an old village with a Romanesque church, and, beyond, the gentle beauty of the Loire landscape.

Hotels and Restaurants
Note: Hotels in the Loire region tend toward the comfortable and friendly rather than the de luxe. A few are former chateaux, often beautifully situated.

Amboise: Hotel Le Choiseul, deluxe in lovely park setting, seasonal, good restaurant; just outside Chateau de Pray, Auberge du Mail, good food.

Angers: Hotels Anjou, Croix de Guerre (good restaurant). Among good restaurants, Le Vert d'Eau.

Blois: Hotels Chateau, Gare et Terminus and Val de Loire, on Tours road below castle.

Chenonceaux: Bon Laboureur Hotel, good restaurant; on Tours road, Ottoni, small, good food.

Chinon: Boule d'Or, river view; Gargantua, small, 15th century former residence, rooms and good restaurant.

Langeais: Duchesse Anne, small, nice garden and good food; Hosten, good restaurant.

Le Mans: Hotels Paris, Central, Moderne, Bec Fin (good restaurant).

Orléans: Hotel Arcades (river view); Ste. Catherine; Moderne. Among many good restaurants: Auberge St. Jacques, La Cremaillere, Jeanne d'Arc, Auberge de la Mantespan (Overlooking river).

Saumur: Bundan, first class hotel; five miles out of town at Chenehutte-les-Tuffeaux is elegant and costly; Les Prieure-Renaissance, set in huge park.

Tours: Hotels Univers, Metropole, the Central, the Bordeaux; restaurants Barrier and Lyonnais. Nearby the super deluxe, 18th century Chateau d'Artigny and the luxurious Chateau-Hotel Domaine de la Tortinere, centuries old mansion set in a private park.

CHAMPAGNE AND BURGUNDY

Two of the great wine regions of France extend from the Ardennes and the Belgian border almost to the outskirts of the bustling city of Lyon. This vast country of vineyards, fields, plains, hills, and valleys also contains some of France's most beautiful cathedrals and interesting abbeys, as well as some exceptionally rich museums and lovely old towns.

Champagne, to the north, was a principal battleground of World War I. Here are Verdun, the Argonne, the Meuse, the Marne, and the battered city of Reims, with its magnificent cathedral now restored.

Champagne's three main grape-producing areas are the Montagne de Reims, the Valley of the Marne, and the Côte des Blancs, all centering around Reims and Epernay. Drives through the area are, in fact, marked out for the motorist in a "champagne route." You may, and should, visit some of the miles-long champagne cellars at Epernay and Reims, and see the old Benedictine Abbey of Hautvillers where the secret of adding the champagne sparkle to still wine was discovered in the 17th century. You will also see the extensive chalk plains, evidence of the unusual subsoil that provides Champagne grapes with their special taste.

Burgundy, to the south, is the home of the powerful dukes who rebelled against the kings of France for centuries. History here can be traced back for 2,500 years—from the Ducal Palace at Dijon, through the 11th- and 12th-century abbeys at Fontenay and Tournus, and the Roman theatre at Lyon, to the 6th-century B.C. Celtic tomb at Chatillon.

Ham, pike, trout, chicken dishes (*poulet au champagne, coq au vin*) are among the regional dishes of Champagne, but its cuisine is rather overshadowed by its sparkling wine. Burgundy, however, has perhaps the finest cuisine in France—Dijon and Lyon are two of the country's major gastronomic centers. You will dine superbly there, as you will also in the hotels and inns in Burgundy's smaller towns and villages. A few of the innumerable specialties are *boeuf bourguignon* (beefstew with wine), frogs' legs, pike (*brochet*), *poulet de Bresse*, artichokes stuffed with goose liver, sausage, gingerbread, spice cake—and of course, Dijon mustard. Among the best known wines are Beaujolais, Chablis, and Beaune. Burgundy is the region where the famous gourmet society called *Confrérie des Tastevins* meets each year for a series of sumptuous banquets. You will easily understand why.

Champagne and Burgundy have much to offer all year round, but the most interesting time to visit them is during September and October, when the grapes are being harvested. In Burgundy, in particular, this is the time of the wine festivals.

The places of interest below are listed in generally north to south order.

Reims, capital of Champagne, has as its glory one of the most famous and magnificent cathedrals in France, where for centuries the kings of France were crowned. Begun early in the 13th century and completed 200 years later, it is a Gothic masterpiece. In the treasury, ornaments and silver used in the coronation ceremonies may be seen. Terribly damaged in World War I, the cathedral has been expertly restored and appears today almost exactly as it did in 1429 when Joan of Arc led the Dauphin here to be crowned Charles VII. In the old Abbey of Saint Denis is the rich Fine Arts Museum, with excellent collections of paintings, tapestries, and a unique assortment of 15th- and 16th-century painted drapings which were used to decorate the town at coronations. In the Modern and Technical College is a monument of far more recent date—the room where the German capitulation was signed on May 7, 1945, kept precisely as it was on that day. From Reims, excursions may be taken to the World War I battlefields. You may also visit the vast wine cellars that range far under the town.

Epernay is the region's other principal "champagne city," with miles of cellars—which may be visited. Nearby, there is a fine view from the Abbey of Hautvillers where Dom Perignon discovered how to add the sparkle to champagne.

Verdun to Bar-le-Duc, both east of Reims, is the "sacred way" which crosses World War I battlefields. Commemorative services are held at Verdun several times during the year.

Troyes was the capital of the Counts of Champagne and owed much of its wealth to its great medieval fairs. Today, it is a city, with many examples of late Gothic architecture, many interesting old streets and houses, and an excellent collection of paintings in its Museum of Fine Arts. At the church of Saint-Jean, Henry V of England married Catherine of France in 1420.

Châtillon-sur-Seine, in Burgundy, has in its museum the "Treasure of Vix," consisting of items that decorated the tomb of a Celtic princess buried more than 2,500 years ago at the nearby village of Vix.

Fontenay is a complete and beautifully preserved 12th-century Cistercian monastery. Though its monks are gone, it is easy to visualize them in the abbey's workshops, mills, forges, bakery, chapter house, cloisters, and enormous vaulted church, all set in a silent, wooded valley.

Bussy-Rabutin is the 17th-century chateau of the Count of Bussy-Rabutin, a clever young man who entertained Louis XIV with his chronicles of court intrigues. When he began to satirize the royal love-life, however, the king exiled him from Paris. Settling here, he built the chateau which has a lovely interior and a fascinating collection of portraits of some 300 of the court personalities whose private lives amused him.

Dijon is the ancient capital of the Dukes of Burgundy, a major art city, and one of the gastronomic capitals of the nation. The Museum of Fine Arts in the Ducal Palace is one of the finest in France, renowned both for the wealth of its collections and for their tasteful arrangement. The sculptured tombs, the Flemish primitives, the Renaissance and medieval art objects are of special interest. The Musée Perrin de Puycousin is devoted to Burgundian folklore. Beautiful churches include Dijon's Notre-Dame, Saint-Michel, and Sainte-Bénigne. Since Dijon is architecturally one of the richest towns in France, you will enjoy exploring the old streets, particularly Rue des Forges. There's plenty to see—if you can get past the restaurants, or as you walk off your meal. In November, Dijon holds its two-week Food Fair. In September, during its Wine Festival, wine literally flows in the Barenzai fountain. Year-round, however, you will dine prodigiously.

Beaune is another great wine center, but most famous for its unique and ancient hospital, the Hôtel-Dieu. Founded in 1450, it is today a modern hospital functioning within surroundings that remain completely medieval, where the customs, rules, and robes of the nuns are exactly as they were 500 years ago. The hospital owns some of the finest vineyards in the area and its annual wine sale attracts buyers from all over the world. Among its other unusual possessions is the masterpiece by Van de Weyden, *The Last Judgment,* in the hospital museum. In the 15th-century residence of the Dukes of Burgundy is a Wine Museum.

Autun is another of Burgundy's eminent art cities, this time with a Roman past. The remains of a temple, a theatre, and a wall are traces of the days when Caesar called Autun "sister and rival of Rome." Of even greater interest, though, are the magnificent 12th century cathedral with some of the finest examples of Romanesque sculpture in France, and the Rolin Museum containing *The Nativity,* a masterpiece of French primitive painting by the Maître de Moulins.

Tournus is a picturesque old town, with many medieval and Renaissance houses, and a splendid 10th-century abbey church.

Cluny was the religious capital of the Christian world in the 11th and 12th centuries, its abbey church, the largest in Europe before the building of St. Peter's in Rome. The part of the transept that remains is perhaps the most beautiful surviving example of the Romanesque period. There are other fine old churches and Romanesque houses.

Mâcon is a center of the wine trade, also famous as the birthplace of the poet Lamartine whose souvenirs abound in this charming old town.

Lyon is a bustling metropolis of 900,000, third largest city in France, center of the silk industry, and, like Dijon, a gastronomic mecca. Essentially a solid, modern, industrial city, it was for four centuries the capital of Roman Gaul. Among reminders of that epoch are a recently excavated Roman theatre and amphitheatre where performances are staged during the summer festival of Lyon-Charbonnières. Thousands also throng to the Lyon Fair in April, an important event in international trade. Lyon's Fine Arts Museum is one of the greatest in France, considered by many experts to be second only to the Louvre. There are also a Museum of Decorative Arts, a remarkable Museum of the History of

Fabrics, a regional historical museum, a museum of Egyptology and Far Eastern arts, and many others. Nearby Charbonnières is a summer resort with racetrack, casino, spa, and restaurants. Also nearby is Pérouges, a beautifully preserved example of a walled medieval town.

Hotels and Restaurants
Hotels in the area are generally quite new and comfortable, though not lavish. Particularly in Burgundy, splendid restaurants abound—large, small, expensive, inexpensive, in cities, towns, villages and hamlets.

Espernay: Hotel Berceaux; Royal Champagne restaurant.

Reims: Hotel Lion d'Or (good restaurant); Hotel Univers and Bristol. Le Florence and La Chaumiere, good food.

Troyes: Hotels Grand and Royal; restaurants Le Champagne, and Le Bourgogne.

Verdun: Hotel Bellevue; Coq Hardi, good restaurants.

Autun: St. Louis et Poste Hotel (good restaurant).

Beaune: Hotel de la Poste; good restaurants are de la Poste and Marche.

Dijon: La Cloche, Hotel Chapeau Rouge (good restaurant) and Central.

Lyon: One of gastronomically great cities in France. Deluxe Hotel Sofitel and its restaurant des Trois Domes; Carlton Royal; Bristol; Le Roosevelt. Restaurants in all price ranges abound. Among well known ones in and around Lyon are Mère Guy, Nandron, and Mère Brazier. Le Reserve at Lissieu is elegant deluxe hotel-restaurant near Lyon. Nearby Paul Bocuse has earned three stars from Michelin for its cuisine and atmosphere.

Tournus: Le Sauvage Hotel; Greuze, good restaurant.

THE EASTERN BORDERS—ALSACE THROUGH THE ALPS

Eastern France is a study in contrasts. From the gentle plateau of Lorraine it rises in three mountain chains, each successively higher, culminating in the spectacular French Alps and Mont Blanc, highest mountain in Europe.

As border country, the northern region has had a frequently turbulent history, Lorraine as battlefield of the Franco-Prussian War of 1870, Alsace as the rich industrial prize. Yet though both provinces have changed hands between France and Germany three times in the past century, they are passionately French—as French as Joan of Arc and the *Marseillaise*, both born here.

Alpine France, with its great university city of Grenoble and world-famous summer and winter resorts of Evian, Aix-les-Bains, Chamonix, Megève, and Courchevel, needs little introduction. But the northern provinces of Alsace and Lorraine are frequently overlooked by the visitor who fears he may see a forest of smokestacks and little else. Yet Nancy and Strasbourg are two of France's most charming cities; the "Joan of Arc country" around Neufchâteau remains almost exactly as it looked in her day; and the border towns between Strasbourg and Mulhouse are among the most picturesque and delightful in Europe, set in the wild and lovely mountains of the Vosges.

Between the Vosges and the Alps lie the green and fertile Jura Mountains, with deep pine forests, trout streams, and pasture lands that produce famous cheeses such as Gruyère, At the center of the region is the beautiful fortified city of Besançon encircled by the River Doubs.

Some of the most interesting and spectacular roads in France are found here. The Wine Route runs from Strasbourg to Mulhouse, winding through the vineyards and picturesque medieval villages of Alsace. The Crest Route, between Colmar and Mulhouse, takes you through the mountains of the Vosges, where views to the Black Forest and Bernese Alps seem worlds away from the industrial preoccupations associated with this coal- and iron-rich province. At St. Julien, you may take the Route of the Alps or the Route of the High Alps. The first follows the

Napoleonic Route taken by the Emperor on his return from Elba. The second is the most spectacular mountain road in Europe, crossing the highest pass accessible to cars.

You will dine well throughout eastern France. In the north, of course, specialties have a German flavor—sauerkraut (choucroute), sausage, excellent beer, fine white wines such as *Riesling* and *Moselle*, delicious liqueurs such as *framboise* and *kirsch*. In Strasbourg you must not fail to sample the *pâté de foie gras*, finest in the world. Besides the famous cheeses, specialties of the Jura are what you would expect to find in green mountain country— trout, mushrooms, crayfish. To appease your appetite sharpened by the Alpine air, there are more cheeses and *fondue* dishes, lake fish, excellent regional wines including *Crepy* and *Seyssel*. Near Grenoble is the home of the famous liqueur *Grande Chartreuse*.

Places of interest are listed below in generally north to south order.

Metz, in northern Lorraine, has two fine churches—a Gothic cathedral with a soaring nave, one of the highest in France, and the 4th-century Saint-Pierre-aux-Nonnains, the country's oldest basilica. Once an important Roman city, Metz has a rich collection of Gallo-Roman antiquities in its Musée Central.

Nancy owes its 18th-century charm to Stanislas Leczinski, King of Poland, and father-in-law of Louis XV. Presented with Lorraine by his royal son-in-law, Stanislas set about beautifying its major city with gracious squares and fountains. Place Stanislas, with its famous wrought iron railings, is one of the city's most beautiful squares, harmonizing with the adjacent Place de la Carrière, equally lovely. The old Ducal Palace contains a museum devoted to the history of Lorraine. Nearby are the towns of Lunéville, with a vast 18th-century chateau built for the Duke of Lorraine, and Baccarat, home of the world-famous crystal.

Neufchâtel, to the southwest, is the center of the Joan of Arc country which extends from Vaucouleurs to Contrexéville. At Domrémy you may see her birthplace and the garden where she first heard her voices.

Strasbourg, capital of Alsace, is one of the most fascinating cities in France, with a superb red sandstone Gothic cathedral, covered bridges, and medieval timbered houses along the canals. You will want to see the cathedral's famous astronomical clock with its animated allegorical figures which pass in review to strike the hours, and the Château des Rohan, home of the infamous Cardinal who involved Marie Antoinette in the "necklace scandal" shortly before the Revolution. Medieval and Renaissance Strasbourg is evoked in the Musée de l'Oeuvre Notre-Dame, and in walks around the old parts of the city, particularly in the section called Petite France. It was in Strasbourg, in 1792, that Rouget de Lisle composed the *Marseillaise,* which acquired its title later when it became the battle song of volunteers from the south of France storming the Tuileries.

Colmar is one of the few European towns that has completely preserved its medieval charm. In addition to its ancient timber-framed and sculptured houses, Colmar has in its cloistered 13th-century Unterlinden monastery one of the most remarkable museums in France. Among its treasures is the Issenheim altarpiece, one of the art marvels of the world. Around Colmar are the picturesque villages of Kaysersberg, Haut-Koenigsbourg, Riquewihr (home of Riesling wine), and Ribeauvillé, "Fiddlers' Town," where there is a delightful festival the first Sunday in September.

Mulhouse, at the other end of the Crest Route, conforms much more closely to the concept of industrial Alsace, but not far away to the west is the village of Ronchamp with its striking (some might say startling) ultra-modern church designed by the famous architect Le Corbusier.

Besançon, a lovely city guarded by an ancient citadel, is the birthplace of Victor Hugo, home of the apéritif *Pernod,* and center of the French watchmaking industry. With ancient churches and old houses, its presents an interesting picture of varied architectural styles. Its museum is particularly rich in drawings.

Morez and **Les Rousses,** almost on the Swiss border, are the principal resorts of the Jura, with good skiing from December to March, fine and scenic climbing and walking during the summer. Farther to the south is the attractive lakeside resort of Nantua, with the huge Genissiat Dam nearby. The Jura resorts offer good food and comfortable lodgings in beautiful surroundings—generally at a price more comfortable than can be found at the more luxurious Alpine resorts in neighboring Savoie.

Evian is one of Savoie's major summer resorts, on the south shore of Lac Leman (Lake Geneva), with all the attractions of a lakeside resort, including a casino, and spas.

Chamonix is the largest, oldest and perhaps most famous of the Alpine resorts in the Mont Blanc area. Both a winter and summer resort, it offers splendid skiing and mountain climbing, as well as an active *après-ski life* for those whose stretch pants will never grace a sitzmark. St. Gervais and Megève are other famous ski (and non-ski) resorts in the area, the last currently considered the most chic.

Aix-les-Bains, like Evian, is a lakeside resort, with spas, casinos, golf.

Courchevel, to the southeast, and nearby Meribel, are comparatively new skiing resorts, fast up-and-coming, popular with skiers of the international set. To the east, at Val d'Isère on the Italian border, is a third famous and spectacular resort in this area. The Alpine skiing season lasts from mid-December to mid-April, extending into May in the high-altitude resorts.

Grenoble is a major city, beautifully situated, with a mountain view at the end of almost every street. Its university is very popular with foreign students, including Americans, and its museum is one of the foremost in France, particularly rich in modern French art. There is also a Stendhal museum with souvenirs of the novelist, who was born here. Above the city is a park reached by telepheric, with scenic views over the country-side. Near Grenoble is the monastery of Grande Chartreuse where the famous liqueur originated. Also near Grenoble is the skiing center of Alpe d'Huez, most important resort area in Dauphine.

Briançon lies near the Col d'Izoard, a striking climatic boundary where Alpine glaciers and forests suddenly give way to Mediterranean landscape, and the road travels through the strange rock cliffs of the Casse Desert. Briançon itself is an old fortified city with ramparts, and a popular winter resort, with ski jumps and a boblsed run.

Hotels and Restaurants

Aix-les-Bains: Leading Hotel Splendide et Royal; Lille is good restaurant on the lake front.

Chamonix: Mont Blanc: Mont Blanc, Croix Blanche, Bellevue (good restaurant) are among leading hotels. (Dozens of small but good hotels dot the ski slopes.)

Colmar: Hotel Bristol; Maison des Tetes, lovely restaurant amid charming medieval atmosphere.

Courchevel: New ski area. Hotels: Carolina and Le Lana. Many charming inns available for ski holidays arranged through travel agents.

Evian: The Royal is elegant with swimming pool, good restaurant; La Verniaz et Les Chàlets has nice setting; Lumina, deluxe resort.

Grenoble: Park Hotel, Trois Dauphins, Savoie and Alpotel are among many good hotels.

Megeve: Mont d'Arbois is plush resort with golf course, heated swimming pool, Rotisserie Grill, snack bars and restaurants; Duc de Savoie and Hermitage, deluxe resort hotels; La Gerentiere good restaurant.

Metz: Hotels: Carlton, Cecil, Royal. Hostellerie de la Marne is good restaurant.

Mulhouse: Parc and Frantel Hotels. Restaurants, Moulin du Kaegy in a lovely old country house.

Nancy: Grand Hotel and its restaurant Stanislas; Hotel Palais; Hotel Excelsior; Hotel Thiers. Restaurants: Rotisserie des Cordeliers and Capucin Gourmand.

Nantua: France and Lyon, both first class hotels each with one star restaurants.

Strasbourg: Hotel Terminus-Gruber and its restaurant le Relais good; Hotel Sofitel (good food). La Chateaubriand, Rotisserie Aubette and Zimmer good restaurants.

SOUTHWESTERN FRANCE— LIMOGES TO THE PYRENEES

Although Biarritz, Lourdes, and Prades are the world-famous objects of pilgrimages of sharply differing natures, many of the riches of southwestern France are as yet relatively undiscovered by foreign visitors. Yet this vast region contains some of the most fascinating sights in France and some of the most colorful customs and people.

Les Eyzies is the capital of prehistory. Cro-Magnon remains of inestimable importance have been found here, and in the nearby caves of Lascaux are superb rock paintings—30,000 years old— that are the finest examples of prehistoric art in Europe, perhaps in the world.

Around Biarritz—if you can tear yourself away from the beach and the casino—is the picturesque Basque Country of bullfights, *pelote*, berets, and fandango dancing. In the wild Gorges of the Tarn is some of France's most dramatic scenery of cliffs, canyons, swirling rivers, and enormous caverns. At Toulouse is the region's great city, a bustling and delightful metropolis of rose-red brick with a wealth of palaces, shrines, and museums. At Carcassonne is one of the most spectacular architectural sights in France—a gigantic fortified city dating from the 6th century to the 13th—completely intact.

The food of the southwestern region is among the country's best. Bordeaux is the home of *bordelaise* sauce, delicious mutton and fish. The great Bordeaux wines are those of the *Medoc, Graves,* and *Sauternes* districts; the greatest perhaps is the white *Château d'Yquem.* Truffles are the specialty of Périgord. From around the Tarn comes Roquefort cheese. Basque country foods include ham and an egg dish called *piperade.* Further east along the Pyrenees and in Toulouse, you will find the casserole specialty called *cassoulet* and the excellent brandy *armagnac,* rival of *cognac* which also comes from southwestern France, north of Bordeaux. In the eastern Pyrenees you will find game— grouse, wild boar, and sometimes bear. Inland, along the rivers and streams, and on the coasts, of course, there is delicious fish. Mushrooms are another specialty of the inland areas.

Limoges is the home of Limoges china, as well as the home of Haviland, originated for American tastes by an American. The fame of its enamel work is even older, and you may visit enamel workers' shops, the porcelain factories, and the Musée Adrien Dubouché, which has rich collections tracing the history of ceramic art. Limoges also has an interesting Gothic cathedral and, in the former Archbishop's Palace, a museum with a wonderful collection of enamels.

Angoulême, west of Limoges, contains the remains of the Chateau d'Angoulême, birthplace of Marguerite of Navarre, sister of Francis I. Perched high on a promontory, its ramparts offer a lovely walk with handsome views. The town is also famous for its chocolates.

Cognac, farther to the west, is the home of the world-famous brandy. The vaulted cellars of Hennessy, Martell, Otard may be visited. The old chateau was the birthplace of Francis I in 1494.

Bordeaux, probably the wine capital of France, is curiously unFrench, perhaps because it was for 300 years an English possession. Capital of the ancient province of Aquitaine, it came under Plantagenet control in 1152 as a result of the marriage of Eleanor of Aquitaine to England's Henry II. An important seaport and flourishing Roman City, Bordeaux provided wine for the tables of the Romans, as well as for the English and the French. Its pride is the huge and richly decorated 18th-century Grand Théâtre, model for the Paris Opera. The Cathedral of St. André is foremost among the many fine churches. The 13th-century Royal Gate was opened only for the passage of sovereigns—Francis I, Charles IX, Louis XIII and Louis XIV. Bordeaux's museums include a Museum of Decorative Arts with notable collections of ceramics, enamels, and metal-works, and a Marine Museum. Vineyards in the neighborhood may be visited. Nearby Arcachon is a coastal resort with beaches and sand dunes, situated on a huge basin.

Périgueux, between Bordeaux and Limoges, is the center of the Périgord region, famous for truffles and fine cuisine, and an excellent excursion center for visiting the prehistoric sites nearby. An interesting city architecturally, Périgueux contains ruins of a Roman temple, a 12th-century Romanesque cathedral with Byzantine pinnacles and cupolas, and medieval and Renaissance houses in the old section around the cathedral. In the museum are excellent prehistoric collections.

Pompadour, northeast of Périgueux, is a village made famous when Louis XV presented its 15th-century chateau and the title Marquise de Pompadour to his favorite, Antoinette Poisson, in 1745. The horse-breeding farm which the king later established here may be visited. It ranks with Haras du Pin in Normandy as the most interesting in France.

Lascaux, southwest of Périgueux, is the center of the extraordinarily rich prehistoric discoveries which extend from Brive to Cabrerets. On the walls of the Lascaux Caves, discovered in

1940, are the most beautiful prehistoric rock paintings in the world. Bulls, horses, deer, bison, even a rhinoceros are drawn with such realism and striking simplicity that they create a frieze of enormous power. Unfortunately, the famous caves of Lascaux are not open to the public now, as the frescoes must be protected from the air as much as possible.

Other interesting and important sites in the region include Les Fyzies, and its rich National Prehistoric Museum; the prehistoric museum at Brive; the wall paintings at Cougnac; and the vast subterranean river of the Gouffre de Padirac.

Albi is a city built of brick, with an exceptional 13th-century fortress-cathedral that provides startling contrast to the cathedrals of northern France. Though the interior is richly decorated, the exterior presents neither a statue nor a bas-relief, but instead the severe ramparts and parapets of an arsenal, which the cathedral was during the bitter years of the religious wars. In the Archbishops' Palace near the cathedral is a museum containing the world's richest collection of paintings, drawings, lithographs, and posters by Toulouse-Lautrec, a native of Albi.

Gorges of the Tarn cut through the countryside northeast of Albi, offering wild and lovely scenery for some 30 miles of crags, rock corridors, cliffs, canyons, and grottos—a geological wonderland that presents quite different aspects when viewed by car and by boat. Millau is the excursion center for the area, which also includes the caves where Roquefort cheese is matured, and which you may visit.

Toulouse is the major city of southwestern France, a bit smaller than Bordeaux, but very French, very lively, very busy. Built of rose-red brick, as is Albi, Toulouse was the literary and artistic capital of southern France during the Middle Ages, and is still a great art city of considerable intellectual prestige. Foremost among its many fine churches is the Basilica of St. Sernin, a masterpiece of 12th-century Romanesque art, exceptionally rich in relics. Along Rue de Metz, Rue des Changes, Rue St. Rome, and neighboring streets are a series of 16th, 17th and 18th century mansions. The Musée des Augustins, in a 14th century monastery, has excellent collections of Romanesque sculpture.

Biarritz is the most fashionable of French Atlantic beach resorts, made famous by Empress Eugénie during the Second Empire, and still going strong, particularly during its high season of July through September. Main attractions are the long promenade, the fine sand beach (king of beaches and beach of kings, they say), and Eugénie's villa, now the Hôtel du Palais. Nearby is the fishing town and resort of St-Jean-de-Luz, with a lively harbor, a fine beach, and interesting old sections. Here, and at Hendaye, on the Spanish border, you are in Basque Country, with its *espadrilles,* whitewashed houses, and dancing in the streets.

Bayonne, a bit inland, is an old and interesting city offering many Basque amusements—the game of *pelote,* bull-fighting, and, during August, festivals with, that's right, dancing in the streets. Bayonne also has a fascinating Basque Museum. In its Musée Bonnat is one of the world's finest collections of drawings. Though Basque Country spills across the border between France and Spain, the Basques are of neither French nor Spanish origin. Their language is unrelated to any other European tongue, and their origin remains mysterious. One of the most intriguing speculations is that they are descendants of survivors of the lost continent of Atlantis.

Pau is a delightful excursion center for the western Pyrenees, blessed with an agreeably mild climate and a splendid valley view, parks and a casino. Napoleon's Marshall Bernadotte, founder of the Swedish dynasty, was born here (there is is an interesting little museum in the house), and France's Henri IV was born in the Château of Pau, where you can see his tortoise shell cradle and a rich collection of tapestries.

Lourdes is probably the most famous place of pilgrimage in the modern Catholic world, drawing more than 2 million visitors each year to its huge basilica and the healing waters of its miraculous

grotto. Here in 1858, 14-year-old Bernadette Soubirous declared
that the Virgin Mary appeared to her in a series of visions, during
one of which a spring miraculously appeared where none had
been before. Pilgrims flocked to the curative spring, the authen-
ticity of the miracle was accepted by the church, Bernadette was
beatified in 1925 and canonized in 1933. The greatest pilgrimages
take place during the third week in August. Pilgrims and
sightseers alike should prepare themselves, however, for the
unfortunate commercialization of the town. Bernadette's birthplace and her father's home may be visited, as may the fine
medieval Château of Lourdes which contains an excellent
museum of the folklore and history of the Pyrenees.

Barèges, south of Lourdes, and nearby *Cauterets,* are popular
Pyrenees winter and summer resort centers, offering skiing,
climbing, camping, hunting. South, at the Cirque de Gavarnie, is
a vast and natural amphitheatre ringed by mountains and dotted
with waterfalls, one of the most beautiful spots in the Pyrenees.

Prades, near Perpignan and the Mediterranean coast, is famous
for its annual music festival honoring Pablo Casals, the great
cellist. Held in July and August, it is probably the most famous of
all the French music festivals. Prades, in the midst of the ancient
and curious province of Roussillon, is a Catalan town, rich in
folklore and Spanish influence.

Perpignan knew its greatest days in the early 14th century as
capital of the kingdom of Majorca, and, later, as a major city of
Catalonia, second only to Barcelona. The Spanish atmosphere
remains, as does the 13th-century palace of the kings of Majorca,
on a summit above the town. At nearby Perthus, Hannibal and his
elephants marched over the Pyrenees. Nearby Banyuls, Col-
lioure, and Argelès are among the picturesque and delightful
beach resorts of the relatively little-known Vermillion Coast.

Carcassonne, to the north, is one of the unforgettable sights of a
trip to France—a magnificently preserved fortified town, dating

mainly from the 6th to 13th centuries. It is the most important and
spectacular feudal city remaining in Europe. Besieged countless
times over the centuries, it was never taken. Charlemagne was
among those who tried—for five years—without success. A
secret of its impregnability was its total self-containment. Forges,
a mill, a mint, a church, even a theatre are within its walls, as well
as ingenious devices designed by Saint Louis and Philippe le
Hardi to foil any intruders so rash as to scale the walls. Though
never taken, Carcassonne was eventually bypassed by more
modern strategies of warfare, to be restored in mid-19th century
by Viollet-le-Duc to its original appearance. Try to see Carcassonne when it is floodlit. At any time, however, this spectacle of
the Middle Ages is breath-taking.

Hotels and Restaurants

Albi: Grand Hotel Vigan, La Reserve Fonvialane (swimming pool
and tennis court).

Arcachon: Regina et Angleterre; Beau Revage at Pyla-Sur-Mer;
Brisants at Pilat-Plage. Corniche is pleasant restaurant at
Pilat-Plage.

Bayonne: Very elegant Chateau de Larraldia, its L'Auberge
restaurant good and deluxe.

Biarritz: Many elegant resort hotels. The Palais and Miramar,
very chic and costly; Plaza Hotel and Regina et Golf, deluxe; the Windsor, moderate. Restaurants: Café de Paris
and de Brindos.

Bordeaux: Splendid hotels and restaurants. Deluxe Royal Gas-
cogne, first class. Restaurants: Clavel, Chateau Trompette,
Reserve Etche Ona (outside of town) and Toque Blanche.

Brive: Hotel du Chapon Fin; Chateau de Castel Novel (ten
minutes outside of Brive—ancient castle in large park,
swimming pool).

Carcassonne: Cite, in the medieval old city; the Hotel Residence et Auter, first class hotel with good restaurant. Logis de Trencavel is one star restaurant.

Les Eyzies: Cro-Magnon Hotel and good restaurant; Les Glycines, good food.

Limoges: The Royal-Limousin Hotel. Le Renoir good restaurant.

Lourdes: Bethanie; Grand Hotel de la Grotte; Ambassadeurs; Imperial; the Moderne. Restaurant: Albert et Taverne de Bigorre.

Pau: Hotel France and Restaurant Cremaillere; Continental Hotel and Le Conti Restaurant, first class; Pierre, good restaurant.

Perigueux: Hotel Domino and Boule d'Or.

Perpignan: Hotel de France and sidewalk restaurant Echanson.

St. Jean de Luz: Hotel de Chantaco in typical basque atmosphere with golf course and tennis court. Restaurant: Petit Grill Basque.

Toulouse: Hotels Les Contes de Toulouse, le Concorde et Rot, and the Grand Hotel et Tivollier, luxury class; Hotel Cie Midi, first class. Le Seville, good restaurant.

PROVENCE AND THE RIVIERA

The south of France is dazzling—there is no other word to describe it. From the cedars and sun-baked yellow plains of Arles to the cypresses and palm-fringed shores of the sparkling Mediterranean, all is color, intensified by the brilliant and unforgettable light of Provence. Hundreds of artists have tried to capture the luminous atmosphere and vivid landscape—Matisse, Cezanne, Van Gogh, Dufy—each adapting it according to his own special vision. But none have been able to improve upon the exotic palette of nature.

When people speak of "the south of France," they refer most

often to the glittering stretch of shore called the *Côte d'Azur* (the Azure Coast) or the Riviera. Geographically, it extends from Marseille to Menton, at the Italian border. But socially it extends only from St. Tropez to Menton, and some would say only from St. Raphaël to Menton, or even Cannes to Menton. This is the land of bougainvillea, yachts, villas, casinos, bikinis, mimosa, magnates, potentates, and starlets. None of it is exactly as it appears either in movies or in the imagination. It is all more so.

But the south of France has other faces which are, according to your tastes, equally or even more intriguing. The Mediterranean region of Provence takes its name from the days when it was called simply "the Roman province." Here are more reminders of the glory of ancient Rome than are to be found anywhere else outside the bounds of Italy. Some even antedate those of Rome, and are more beautiful, and even more beautifully preserved. Orange, Arles, Vienne, and Nîmes have spectacular Roman souvenirs in their theatres, temples, and arenas, and the Pont du Gard (which is really an aqueduct, not a bridge), one of the most magnificent of Roman achievements.

The south of France is also extremely rich in modern art and architecture, not only in the museums of Antibes, Biot, Cagnes, Menton, Nice, and St. Tropez, but also in the living art of Le Corbusier's "Radiant City" at Marseille and in Matisse's chapel at Vence.

As you drive along one of the Riviera's breath-taking Corniche roads, if you will draw your gaze away from the sea and look to the north, you will realize that just beyond the Azure Coast is a string of wild mountain peaks, glittering with snow in the Mediterranean sun. The snowfields and slopes of Auron and Valberg, in the Alpes-Maritimes, offer skiing from November to April, only 60 miles from the palm trees of Nice.

Southern France is a vacationer's paradise, whether you incline toward skiing, skin diving, gambling, sight-seeing, or girl-watching. It offers its pleasures at all prices, provided you are willing to do a bit of research. The luxury hotels and restaurants can be fantastically expensive. In the same resorts, a few blocks away, are more modest, but more than adequate establishments where you will feel no pain other than your sunburn.

A few facts of Riviera life may be helpful. If you are more

interested in scenery, swimming, sunbathing, and a bit of peace and quiet than you are in ogling the real and would-be international set, try coming in the off-season (May, June or September), or try one of the resorts west of St. Tropez to Hyères. Though they can scarcely be called undiscovered, they are generally a bit less crowded. Their beaches, oddly enough, are, on the whole, far better than those of the best-known resorts. From Menton to Nice, the beaches are rock or pebble. From Antibes to Cannes, the beaches are sand, but very small. From Cannes to St. Raphaël, they are rocky. From St. Raphaël and St. Tropez to Hyères, they are sandy and very pleasant indeed.

Water sports of every description are available. Your evening entertainment may be as elegant, or as gaudy, or as peaceful, as your taste dictates or your pocketbook decrees.

In all of the south of France, you will eat extremely well. Some of the country's most famous restaurants are here, notably in Vienne and Les Baux. As you approach the Mediterranean, you will find southern influence appearing, in olives, oil, and garlic, the last particularly apparent in any dish called *provençal*. This is country for artichokes, eggplant, tomatoes, zucchini, fish. The great regional specialty is fish stew, at its most famous in the *bouillabaisse* of Marseille, which depends largely on a Mediterranean fish called *rascasse*, and in which you may or may not find the heads of fish included, depending on the pretensions of your dining establishment. Try it anyway. Other specialties include cod, *salade niçoise*, and, for the adventurous, octopus and baby octopus. Local fruits include oranges, figs, and tangerines. Famous wines of northern Provence are *Tavel* and *Châteauneuf du Pape*. To the south, the local *rosés* are good, although almost any restaurant can produce whatever wine you'd like, for a price, of course.

Vienne is far to the north, just south of Lyon in fact, but spiritually a part of Provence, because Roman France begins here in earnest. There is a Roman theatre and a beautifully preserved Temple of Augustus, as well as some fascinating medieval houses, still lived in, but looking exactly as they did three and four hundred years ago. Pride of Vienne, however, is the restaurant Pyramide, perhaps the most famous restaurant in the world.

Orange contains a great Roman theatre where, in July, you may see drama, dance, and musical performances in the setting of the Romans of 1,800 years ago. Certainly the finest of its kind in Provence, the theatre is considered by many experts to be the finest example of its kind anywhere in the world. The Triumphal Arch of Tiberius, dating from about the same time, is also remarkably preserved, and decorated with sculpture representing trophies, battle scenes, and floral designs.

Avignon was the city of the popes and the anti-popes for 100 years in the 14th century. The magnificent Palace of the Popes remains, its ramparts enclosing chapels, vaulted halls, cloisters, and gardens, in an immense and seemingly endless fortress-residence that dominates the city. A drama festival takes place here in July. Also to be seen are the tiny, ancient streets around the palace, the city ramparts, beautiful churches, and medieval homes of the cardinals. In this undeniably fascinating and delightful city a myth may be demolished for you, however. The Pont d'Avignon of the childhood song still exists, but its real name is Pont Saint-Benezet, and one danced under (*sous*) and not on (*sur*) it. Near Avignon is the medieval town of Vaison-la-Romaine, interesting both for its 12th-century castle and the extensive remains of a Roman city with a bridge, theatre, houses, paved streets, mosaics, baths—almost as complete as Pompeii, though smaller.

Nîmes is the oldest of the Roman cities of Gaul, with an unusual series of buildings and monuments which rival even those of Rome. Its 1st-century arena could hold more than 20,000 spectators and is the best preserved of those which remain today. Bullfights are often held here now, generally the French kind, in which the bull is not killed. The Maison Carrée, one of the most beautiful of Roman buildings, is now a museum with an outstanding collection of medals and Gallo-Roman antiquities. The Temple of Diana, the Thermes (transformed into gardens), and the Tour Magne, from which you may glimpse the sea on a clear day, are among the city's Roman treasures. Nearby is the Pont du Gard, the most impressive of all Roman monuments in Gaul. Constructed in 19 B.C. to bring spring waters to Nîmes, it consists of three superimposed series of arches, of which the topmost carried the water. Built as a purely utilitarian aqueduct, it is nevertheless a masterpiece of architecture. Nîmes is not, however, content to contemplate its past. It is also a bustling commercial and industrial city.

Arles was an important Roman city, and under the Emperor Constantine became, after Constantinople, the second capital of the empire. Its great arena is larger than that at Nîmes, though less well preserved, and also provides an impressive setting for bullfights during the summer season. Only columns and piles of stone indicate what was once the fine Roman theatre, but the ancient sarcophagi of the Roman necropolis still line the avenue of the Alyscamps. Near Arles are some of the most intriguing country sights of Provence, among them St. Rémy and Les Baux. At Les Antiques, in St. Rémy, are excavations of the ancient Gallo-Roman city of Glanum, and of an even earlier Gallo-Greek city. Also at St. Rémy is the priory that sheltered Vincent van Gogh, where he painted many of his tormented masterpieces.

Les Baux, once an important medieval town, now a magnificent ruin, is perched on gigantic rocks from which there is the most awesome view in all Provence. Wandering through its streets, you will come upon haphazard houses hewn from the rock, crumbling chapels, remnants of the castle which knew a brilliant life in the 13th century. Each Christmas eve, there is an unforgettable midnight mass at Les Baux, when, by candlelight and to the music of fife and drum, shepherds bring their lambs in offering. However, Les Baux is also the site of more worldly attractions. Its restaurant, La Baumanière, a bit down the slope, is one of the finest in France, complete with swimming pool.

Aix-en-Provence is the place to go if the past of Provence is too much with you. It has its past, too, of course, but today appears as a quiet, gracious, and charming 17th- and 18th-century city with spacious café-lined avenues and lovely fountains. The studio of Cézanne is here, and an excellent fine arts museum, as well as an excellent tapestry museum.

Marseille is bursting with the animation and color of the Mediterranean. It is the second largest city in France, and the oldest, with a history that goes back 2,500 years, flourishing through French, Visigoth, Roman, Celtic, and Greek domination, its fame and desirability always centering around its port. The past, however, receives barely a nod these days, particularly since the Old Port area was blown up by the Nazis in 1943. The people of Marseille are its main attraction, best observed from the cafés of its famous street, La Canebière, which leads to the port. There are several good museums, but you should make a special effort to see the modern complex of apartments called La Cité Radieuse, designed by Le Corbusier, in keeping with the dynamism of the city. Should you insist on a bit of history, you may take a boat from the Quai des Belges to Château d'If. The castle was built by Francis I in the 16th century, but its greatest fame as prison of Dumas' *Count of Monte Cristo* is, alas, pseudo-history. Marseille is a wonderful, brawling, lusty city—like its *bouillabaisse,* unique, though it may or may not be to your taste.

Camargue. West of Marseille, in the delta of the Rhône, is one of the most curious areas in France, a marshy prairie called the Camargue. Here, surrounded by tall grass, egrets, flamingos, and ibis, French-style cowboys tend herds of sheep, cattle, and ponies. As if this were not unusual enough, at the Camargue town of Saintes-Maries-de-la-Mer, gypsies from throughout the world gather each year, in May, to honor their patron saint, Sarah, who, according to legend, landed here in 40 A.D. with her mistress Mary Salome, sister of the Virgin Mary, and mother of two of the apostles.

Toulon is France's most important naval base, and, as such, suffered heavily during World War II. It is still the great base for the French Mediterranean fleet, its roadstead filled with warships, its streets thronged with sailors.

Hyères, though outside the bounds of the more social and frequently more frenzied sphere of the Riviera proper, is the oldest of French Mediterranean resorts. Well established by the British in the 18th century, it is still a picturesque and charming resort, with many beaches. Excursions may be made to the delightful Iles de Hyères. The largest, Porquerolles, offers a particularly gentle climate, lavish vegetation, excellent sand beaches.

St. Tropez has long been a favorite resort for artists and writers. It is something of a Riviera extension of St-Germain-des-Pres, but very young and very gay, with undeniable charm and attractions. Among them are the old houses and twisting streets of its Vieux Port, its citadel, its early-summer festivals. It is often very crowded, but no one seems to mind.

St. Raphaël prides itself on being "the resort where the Côte d'Azur beings." It is highly popular, a bit on the family side, and well endowed with hotels and a good beach.

Cannes, undoubtedly the social and spiritual capital of the Riviera, will conform to all your ideas of what the Riviera should be. There are two casinos, a colorful port shared by fishing boats and luxury yachts, lavish hotels along the Promenade de la Croisette, and enough festivals to keep you from noticing that the beach is as skimpy as the bikinis. Most famous of the goings-on is the International Film Festival held during the first two weeks in May. There is a splendid view from Super-Cannes, above the city. In the hills, a short distance to the north is the town of Grasse, world capital of the perfume industry. More than 87,000 acres of fields supply Grasse with its flower petals to be made into perfume. To give some idea of the staggering amount of flowers

used—12,000 pounds of roses make one pound of perfume
essence, 1,000 roses weigh less than 2 pounds. You may, of
course, visit a perfume factory, but you must rely on your own
judgment in deciding whether the unlabelled or code-labelled
perfumes you can buy here are really the great bargains that they
seem.

Juan-les-Pins has a casino and a good beach, but tends more
toward brassy than elegant.

Cap d'Antibes, its next-door neighbor, is precisely the opposite.
Its luxurious Hôtel du Cap and Eden Roc restaurant draw some
of the wealthiest people in the world, in search of a bit of
expensive semi-seclusion. Antibes itself is a more popular resort,
with a small museum in the Grimaldi castle, devoted chiefly to
paintings, ceramics, and lithographs by Picasso. At Cagnes,
nearby, is the house where Renoir spent the last years of his life.

Vence, in the hills between Antibes and Nice, is the site of the
famous chapel decorated by Matisse. A short distance away, at
Biot, is the Fernand Leger Museum, fronted with a striking
mosaic. Art lover or not, you will, in fact, find the Riviera
hinterland worth exploring for its glimpses of villas and breath-
taking panoramas of the sea.

Eze, an old fortified town, clinging to the side of a cliff. Exploring
its narrow, winding streets is a memorable experience.

Nice may come as a surprise, because it is a good-sized city as
well as an internationally famous resort. Swimming and sunbathing are not the major attractions of Nice. Instead one comes to
enjoy its great seafront Promenade des Anglais, its casino, flower
market, nightclubs, and almost continuous sports events and
festivals. Most famous is its stupendous Carnival during the two
weeks preceding Lent. Though it has an excellent climate and
beautiful location, and perhaps the most famous name along the
Riviera, Nice tends to draw a somewhat less elegant and less

sportif crowd than its smaller neighbors. From Nice to the Italian border, the coast is dotted with villas, superb views, and gems of resorts, among them Cap Ferrat, Eze, Cap d'Ail, Menton.

Monaco is a principality, a sovereign state, and a world unto itself. In this 370-acre country (smaller than New York's Central Park) are crowded (and perched, for it is all up-and-down) four towns, a palace, and the world-famous Monte Carlo casino. The Monegasques enjoy two fairy-tale distinctions: they pay no taxes, and they have Grace Kelly as their princess. Sole drawback of their nationality is that they may not enter the game rooms of the Casino, though others, who have nursed the fantasy of "breaking the bank," may not consider this a drawback. In Monaco, you will want to visit the Oceanographic Museum, one of the finest in the world.

Hotels and Restaurants
Unless you're traveling extremely casually and are willing to accept any sort of potluck, it's important to nail down your Riviera reservations in advance. As you check in, nail down the exact price of your accommodations, too, service and all, to avoid unpleasant surprises.

Vienne: Deluxe Hotel—La Residence de la Pyramide; moderate priced hotels, Nord and Central. The celebrated three-star restaurant Pyramide (reservations absolutely necessary). Bec Fin and Chez René are both good restaurants.

Orange: Hotels Arene and Princes good in moderate price range. The Arene restaurant and the Provencal restaurant have been awarded one star each by the prestigious Michelin.

Avignon: The Europe Hotel in the deluxe class (good restaurant); the Hiely and Auberge de France, good food; the Le Prieure Hotel (nearby at Villeneuve-les-Avignon) deluxe. Only seven miles out of Avignon is the well known Auberge de Noves Hotel with a two star restaurant.

Nîmes: Hotel Imperator, deluxe, and Cheval Blanc, first class hotel; Le Lisita, La Louve, La Pergola and Chez Maitre Itier, comfortable restaurants.

Arles: Jules César Hotel and Restaurant Lou Marques, good; also Hotel Nord Pinus.

Aix-en-Provence: Hotel Roy Rene, deluxe and good restaurant; Riviera "Le Pigonnet" on the Marseille road, first class hotel with good restaurant.

Marseille: Concorde-Prado, Grand Hotel et Noailles, Splendide, L'Arbois, Beauvan, deluxe; hotels Astoria and Castellane, first class. Among the many excellent restaurants are New York, Jambon de Parme, Calypso, Michel, Brasserie des Catalans. (Bouillabaisse is a famed fish dish and should be enjoyed during a stay in Marseille. Many restaurants have lovely views of the sea.)

Les Baux-Des-Provence: About two hours outside of Marseille— La Baumanière, is one of the few three star restaurants in France according to the prestigious Michelin, worthy of a detour to visit. (Advance reservations essential.) La Baumanière, also has a swimming pool, tennis courts and a spectacular view of the valley below. La Cabro d'Or and La Riboto de Taven are less expensive but excellent.

Menton: Hotels Napoleon, Royal, Westminster, Viking, Parc and Price de Galles, all first class. Restaurants: Roc-Amadour, Chez Mireille and Hotel Ermitage.

St. Tropez: Byhlos and la Pinede, very elegant and costly beach resort hotels; Lei Mouscardins and Auberge des Maures, well known restaurants.

St. Raphael: Hotels Beau Sejour and the Continental; La Voile d'Or restaurant.

Cannes: The lavish Majestic Hotel, the Carlton, Marinez, Grand, Gray d'Albion and Miramar are hotels in the elegant category but many others in Cannes or nearby are in moderate range. (Reservations far in advance a must for the glamorous Riviera resort in season.)

Juan-les-Pins: Hotels Provencal, Belles Rives, Juana. Restaurant: Bijou Plage.

Cap-D'Antibes: The renowned Hotel du Cap and the Eden Roc are the elegant habitats of the famous and wealthy. Down a notch, the Residence du Cap.

Nice: Negresco, one of France's most elegant and distinguished resort hotels. Plaza, Splendid, Sofitel, Park and Napoleon, plus scores of others, nicely located. Perigord, Petit Brouant, La Poularde chez Lucullus, among top restaurants.

Monaco: Hotel Paris (good restaurant);Metropole and Hermitage, deluxe. Restaurants: Chapon Fin, Bec Rouge and Casino. Lovely resorts and restaurants are dotted along the scenic and glamorous French Riviera.